Backyard Bouquets

Backyard Bouquets

Growing Great Flowers for Simple Arrangements

by Georgeanne Brennan

Photography by Kathryn Kleinman

Flower Styling by Ethel Brennan

CHRONICLE BOOKS

SAN FRANCISCO

Library of Congress Cataloging-in-Publication Data available.

ISBN 0-8118-1413-0

Printed in Hong Kong.

Edited by Sharon Silva
Book and cover design by Gretchen Scoble

Distributed in Canada by Raincoast Books
8680 Cambie Street
Vancouver, British Columbia V6P 6M9

10 9 8 7 6 5 4 3 2 1

Chronicle Books
85 Second Street
San Francisco, California 94105

Web Site: www.chronbooks.com

Contents

Introduction

THIS IS A BOOK ABOUT GROWING FLOWERS TO CREATE BOUQUETS. IT IS NOT NECESSARY to have a proper cutting garden to have vasefuls of lovely home-grown blossoms. The planting of a single packet of sunflower seeds or a dozen daffodil bulbs can realize the goal. The intent of this volume is to encourage the ease and satisfaction of growing simple flowers, whether a single plant in the most limited space or many different blooms in a large garden. In either instance, mixing your own flowers together with seasonal elements gathered from the surrounding landscape or purchased from farmers' markets or florists will provide infinite combinations for bouquets. Whatever is in season is suitable. In spring, branches from flowering fruit trees and lilac bushes can be combined with the early bulbs, while summer brings wild grasses, berries, roses, and hydrangeas for adding to cuttings of sunflowers, zinnias, and sprays of coreopsis.

Although any flower can be admired in the overall scheme of the landscape, in this book enhancing and beautifying the garden plot becomes secondary to satisfying the passion for having a house full of bouquets. Thus, tulips are planted so that most of them can be cut just as they crack and their languorous opening enjoyed daily at close proximity, rather than leaving them in the garden to be admired by the occasional passerby. A terra-cotta pot sitting on your porch, brimful with a hundred tulips, is a splendid sight, but well over half of the stems can be cut in bud and brought inside without the planting looking decimated.

All of the flowers, most of them annuals, that I have chosen to include grow quickly and easily, and require no special skills, equipment, or environmental conditions to ensure cut flowers for bouquets. Only adequate sunlight, water, healthy soil, and fertilizer are needed. Some of the flowers are planted in fall for spring flowering, others in spring to flower in summer and on into fall. A few can be planted in midsummer for fall bloom.

The flowers are grouped in chapters according to their aesthetic similarities, with the exception of poppies and lupines, which are paired because they flower at the same time in the wild. The brightly colored, round-faced, sometimes domed blooms of the cosmos, coreopsis, zinnia, and the sunflower are collected in one chapter. Small flowers with masses of visually interesting foliage such as Queen Anne's lace and love-in-a-mist, the so-called filler flowers, are united in another. Vines are the defining motif for the chapter on sweet peas and nasturtiums, and it is the stiff uprightness of dahlias and irises that determines their chapter. Tulips, daffodils, and ranunculuses share a gracefulness of form that aesthetically sets them apart as a group.

After a brief introduction, each chapter presents an overview of the characteristics of the particular flowers, the general types that are available, and specific planting, growing, and harvesting information. A selection of different varieties follows, with details on the size of the flower heads, the height and growth habit of the plant, and the suitability for container growing. Scattered throughout the chapters is additional garden information such as saving seeds of sunflowers and sweet peas, and digging and dividing iris and dahlia tubers. You will also find brief descriptions of flower-arranging tools and how they work, such as frogs, marbles, and floral foam; flower-preserving solutions; suggestions for bouquet making; and seasonal suggestions for flowering shrubs and trees to combine with your garden flowers.

These chapters are prefaced by a short section on starting a garden both in place and in containers, including what to do about pests and diseases that might attack your efforts.

A final section, consisting of suggested content and design for three simple backyard bouquet gardens, follows the flower chapters.

In the Garden

IN THIS CHAPTER ALL THE ELEMENTS NECESSARY TO GROW FLOWERS SUCCESSFULLY ARE discussed, enabling the enthusiastic flower-lover to get into the garden as soon as possible. First to be considered is location and soil, followed by the preparation of the site. Once the ground is prepared, three aspects of seeding are presented: direct seeding, starting seeds indoors, and transplanting seedlings. Of course, once the garden has been planted, it is time to consider maintenance, and this appears next in the chapter under the headings watering, fertilizing, and pests and diseases. Finally, for those who lack a garden space or wish to grow flowers in containers, there is a final section, growing in containers.

LOCATION

Flowers, like most other plants, require sun, water, and nutrients to grow and to bloom. The first thing to think about is location, even if you are only going to grow a trellis of sweet peas in spring or a summer plot of dahlias. Most of the flowers in this book require a location with at least three-quarters of a day of full sun, and preferably an entire day. If you have no garden area that meets this requirement, consider growing your bouquet flowers in containers that can be placed on a sunny patio, porch, or balcony.

Water should be readily accessible. Although it is possible to fill and carry watering cans, a garden hose that reaches to your planting area is more convenient, and your plants are far more likely to receive the water they need.

SOIL

Soils, which are composed of particles of sand, silt, and clay, plus organic matter, vary considerably in quality. An ideal soil, a loam, has about equal proportions of the three particles, plus maybe 5 percent organic matter, and is neither too acidic nor too alkaline, that is, has a pH between 6 and 7. (Simple kits for testing the soil pH are available at nurserys and garden centers.) Water and air can move easily through loam, yet sufficient water and nutrients are held in the plant's root zone. Few of us have this ideal soil, so amending with large amounts of organic material is the easiest solution. Adding manure, compost, or other organic material increases the pore spaces in heavy clay soil or silt soil, allowing the passage of air and water. In sandy soils, which already drain well, or too well, the organic matter will reduce the pore space and provide holding sites for nutrients. Organic matter in soil decomposes over time, so it is important to remember that not only does it need to be replaced yearly, but since the process of decomposition uses nitrogen from the soil, nitrogen fertilizer requirements are greater for plants growing in soils with a high organic content.

Generally speaking, soils in areas with high rainfall are acidic and those in arid regions are alkaline, because high evaporation brings salts to the surface and rain washes them back down. The addition of lime to acidic soils reduces the acidity, and the addition of sulfur (usually as calcium sulfate, called gypsum) reduces alkalinity. Both high acidity and high alkalinity are detrimental to almost all plants. Both can be improved or amended if necessary.

PREPARATION

The first step in preparing your garden for planting is to remove the weeds and weed seeds. If the ground is dry, water your site several days to a week before beginning to plant, as it is much easier to work moist soil. It should not, however, be wet. Cut and remove the large weeds, then dig down about one foot and turn the soil over to aerate it, breaking up large clods and mixing in any amendments and a balanced fertilizer. The soil should be worked into a good seed bed, without large clods, so that water will be held in the immediate area of the germinating seed, and the new seedling and its roots can easily emerge. If you have the time, water again lightly before planting your flower seeds. This will start the weed seeds that have been freshly brought to the surface. A week or so after watering, many of these seeds will have germinated and can be removed by hoeing. You can now plant your flower seeds directly into the moist subsoil where they can germinate without a new watering, which could also start new weeds that would compete with the emerging seedlings for space and light. When the seedlings need their first watering, they will be ahead of the weeds that the watering will germinate.

Direct Seeding

Nearly all the nonbulbing flowers in this book are readily grown by planting seeds directly into the garden. Pay close attention to the recommended planting depths, as a small seed may not have the energy reserves to emerge if sown too deeply, and a large seed, which requires a greater amount of water to germinate than small seeds, may dry out if planted too shallowly.

Starting Seeds Indoors

In areas with short growing seasons, seeds can be started indoors in flats or small pots approximately six weeks before the last local frost date, then later transplanted outside. To do this, fill small pots or seedling trays with a potting mix and soak the potting mix until it settles, adding more soil if necessary and moistening it as well. Plant the seeds to the specified depth, then place the trays or pots in a warm place—65 to 75 degrees F—until the seeds germinate and produce their first two leaves, the cotyledon leaves. At this point, the seedlings will need sunlight and fertilizer to grow. If a sunny spot is impossible, grow lights can provide the necessary light. Apply a dilute liquid fertilizer weekly.

TRANSPLANTING SEEDLINGS

Transplants should be planted out before the plants' roots have become cramped in the tray or pot and twisted into a tangle. They are ready to be shifted outside when their roots can hold the soil ball together but are not yet confined. Lift a plant by the stem: if the soil mix comes cleanly with the roots, the plant is ready to be moved. If a plant is left in the tray or small pot, the roots will grow in a circle out to the edge of the container and become root bound. Such plants often do not grow readily after transplanting because their roots never reach straight out into the soil.

If you are buying transplants, don't just choose the largest ones. Lift the plants and check the bottoms to avoid buying root-bound specimens, which the larger ones often are. Once in the soil, the smaller plants will quickly catch up to and often surpass those that are root bound. Next, look for sturdiness in stems and branches, and deep, even color.

Before planting, soak the seedlings, still in their trays or pots, in a sink or bucket until the potting mix is saturated; that way, the seedlings can be removed easily from their containers without damaging their roots. While the seedlings are soaking, prepare a hole for each one. Remove each seedling, keeping the root ball intact, and put it in the prepared hole, covering the roots well. Then fill the hole with soil, tamping it around the roots. Using a gently sprinkling hose or watering can, water the soil around the seedlings.

WATERING

For plants to grow well, the soil should be neither too wet nor too dry. Very wet soil has its pore spaces filled with water instead of air, seriously limiting the amount of oxygen available to the roots. After the pore spaces drain, the remaining water is held by the soil particles. At first the water is easily removed by the plant's roots, but as less and less remains, it is more tightly held to the soil particles and a tremendous amount of physical effort is required from the plants to dislodge it. Consequently, plants in dry soils have to expend large amounts of the energy manufactured by their leaves to acquire water rather than to promote growth. At some point of dryness, the soil's ability to hold the water exceeds the plant's ability to lift it, and at that point the plant wilts.

Ideally the soil is slightly moist but not soggy, and watering should only put back into the root zone the amount of water the plant has used. In hot, windy periods, the plant will obviously use more water than when it is cold and foggy, so watering should occur more often during these drying times. Looking at the surface of the soil is no guide to deciding when to water. The plant's roots fill an area underneath the surface, so it is important to dig into the root zone and look at the moisture levels around the roots before watering. After doing this through different seasons, you will have a better idea of an appropriate watering schedule.

Newly planted seeds need water to begin the enzyme systems that initiate growth. Since the seeds have no roots and new seedlings have only small roots, it is important that moisture be readily available to them throughout germination and early growth.

If a seed is allowed to dry after germination has begun, the embryonic seedling will dry and die. Likewise, overwatering seeds and seedlings can cause rot and fungus that are often fatal, or it can suffocate small root systems.

FERTILIZING

Fertilizing provides the elements necessary for plant growth. As plants grow, they extract the elements they need for their growth from the soil. Adding fertilizer makes these elements abundant and available. The most essential of them are nitrogen, phosphorus, and potassium (N, P, and K, respectively). Common commercial fertilizers list the percentages of N, P, and K in that order, for example, 21–12–8. A balanced fertilizer will have about equal amounts of the three. Minor elements are also required for plant growth and can be added as needed from commercial fertilizers. Some of them may already be in the soil, but the great variation in soil types precludes predictions. For detailed information about your specific soil, it is best to check with a local expert such as an extension agent or nurseryperson. Overfertilizing can severely damage a plant, scorching its leaves and sometimes even killing it, so it is wise to add a dilute fertilizer over a period of time rather than a strong fertilizer once, especially on young plants.

Plant growth starts slowly, then moves to a much higher rate before flowering, as the plant vigorously adds leaves and stems. After this point, it slows again. The nutrients from fertilizer need to be available to or already in the plant during the rapid growth stage, so fertilizing should occur before it happens. Granular fertilizers often need to be reduced to soluble forms by soil bacteria before they can be taken up by the roots, so time also should be allowed for this process. Generally, however, liquid fertilizers are available immediately to the plant.

Organic fertilizers, like manures, have relatively low nitrogen levels, in the 3 percent to 6 percent range, and a large amount of organic matter that actually consumes nitrogen in its decomposition process. The decomposition may not leave much nitrogen free for the plants' needs; however, the manures add other elements and cause good tilth and soil health.

Plants in containers are fairly captive and are outside the soil dynamics of the garden, so it is necessary to fertilize them more often, usually once a week, preferably with a dilute liquid fertilizer.

Since nitrogen is the element most heavily used in plant growth, it can serve as an indicator of plant nutrition—but only an indicator.

PESTS AND DISEASES

There is a wide array of pests and diseases that attack flowers, and there is a wide array of responses. The problems vary from species to species, region to region, and season to season, and the responses vary from person to person. Some gardeners are reluctant to use chemical controls, relying on those of botanical origin only, while others have no qualms about applying chemicals. Such choices are not necessarily right or wrong, although some may be more effective than others.

The plants in this book are relatively sturdy, robust, and easy to grow, but they can be beset by pests and disease nonetheless. The considerable regional variations make a single solution impossible, however, so it is advisable to contact a knowledgeable local person, such as a farm advisor or nurseryperson, for specific remedies to any problems.

GROWING IN CONTAINERS

Plants in containers need to be looked after more than plants in the ground do, but they are a good option if climate, soil, or space limit your garden.

Containers must have a drainage hole in the bottom and must be filled with a soil mix that drains readily. While a soggy mix will cause root rot and eventually kill the plants, too much drainage will quickly remove water and fertilizer from the already small root zone. Commercial soil mixes for containers are usually composed mostly of organic matter, like bark or compost with some peat moss, so adding sand or perlite, if it isn't already present, will increase drainage, which is critical to the health of the plant.

Once you have selected the correct-sized container for your planting, that is, one that will have adequate space for the roots to grow and mature, cover the drainage hole in the bottom with a layer of gravel or a few small rocks. Moisten the potting mix, then fill the container to within one inch of the rim for most seeds or plants. Sow seeds according to the instructions given in individual plant descriptions. For transplants, make a hole in the potting mix large enough for the root ball and pack with moist potting mix.

Since container plants often have smaller root systems, they may need to be watered more often than garden plants. With that in mind, though, they should be watered on about the same schedule as garden plants are. Specifically, they need more water when they are actively growing or in hot and windy weather, and less water when they are in a quiet phase or the weather is cooler. Again, it is important to look at the soil under the surface, not on the surface, to make watering decisions.

Fertilize container plants either lightly and often with a dilute fertilizer or, if perennials, a few times a year with a slow-release product. A heavy dose of strong fertilizer concentrated in the confines of a container will burn roots and leaves. As with water, the plants should have more fertilizer during periods of active, vigorous growth and less when they are dormant or growing slowly.

Disks and Domes
Sunflower, Zinnia, Cosmos, Coreopsis,
and Pincushion Flower

Disks and Domes

BOUQUETS OF SUNFLOWERS, ZINNIAS, COSMOS, COREOPSIS, AND PINCUSHION FLOWERS, IN a rainbow of brilliant colors from rusty gold to shocking pink to delicate mauve, can be gathered from summer until the plants are shriveled by the frosts of late fall. These flowers are typically grown from seed sown in spring and early summer, although in the Mediterranean climate of Northern California, where I live, I can have cut sunflowers and zinnias for Thanksgiving from seeds I planted in late August. When sown in a garden spot of warm soil in a location with full sun, or nearly so, and supplied with adequate moisture, sunflower and zinnia seedlings will appear in four or five days—just the sort of precocity an impatient gardener loves—and some varieties reward the grower with the first flowers for cutting within six weeks.

With the exception of the domelike pincushion flower, which belongs to the Dipsacaceae family, all the rest are members of the sunflower tribe, a subgroup in the Compositae family distinguished by the composition of their flowers: many small florets surrounded by an outer row of florets with ray petals around a central disk. Annuals all, these profusely blooming flowers are among those our great-great-grandparents laid claim to in cottage gardens across the country, prompting their common description of being old-fashioned flowers. Other than some of the sunflowers that produce only one bloom per stalk, all the plants continue to grow and to bloom repeatedly, so cutting the flowers initiates more growth and more blossoms.

Not only do these colorful summer disks and domes bloom over a long period of time, but once cut, they also are long lasting, with most of them keeping their beauty for seven days. That longevity, combined with the rapidity of their growth, their abundance in the garden, and their ease of care make them outstanding candidates for bouquet growing for even the gardening novice.

SUNFLOWER

Bright and cheerful, sunflowers are among the easiest of flowers to grow. Although the typical bloom is yellow petals with a dark brown center, many variations exist in the sunflower world. Colors range from deep rust-red to nearly white, sizes from dinner plate to espresso saucer, height from eighteen inches to eight feet, and form from a single stalk to branching. Personally, I am enamored of the rusty red, pinkish brown, and pale cream branching sunflowers that, throughout their season, produce both large, thick-stalked flowers from the center and smaller, thinner-stalked ones from the side shoots. It is rather like having two plants in one. The thin-stemmed ones can be used in small tabletop bouquets, on their own, or in mixed bunches. The nonbranching varieties that produce only a single, sturdy stem for a one-time cutting generally bloom all together, but they can be sown in successive plantings for flowers all summer long.

The florets of the sunflower ripen in a clockwise circular pattern from outside in, in the course of which they shed their bright yellow pollen, often leaving little circlets on a table or floor when in bouquets. Nonshedding varieties, which are male-sterile and consequently produce no pollen to shed, are now available for cut flowers. Sunflower seeds are so varied that putting them next to one another can cause you to wonder if they are all really sunflowers or if some other seed has inadvertently been mixed in. The familiar black-and-white-striped seeds can be as large as a thumbnail or as small as a pencil tip. Many of the other seeds are black, brown, white, or striped. In the case of 'Autumn Beauty' and 'Evening Sun,' the small seeds are a mixture of colors.

Regardless of the size and shape of the seeds, plant all of them in the same fashion, in a location that receives at least three-quarters to a full day of sun. Sunflowers that do not receive adequate sunlight will have spindly, weak stems and small blooms. Sow them one-half inch deep in moist, prepared ground, nine to twelve inches apart for the full-sized varieties, and six to nine inches apart for the dwarf types, those that are two feet or less. In areas with mild winters, sow them from March through

In Season

Roses, berries, grapevines, flowering myrtle, viburnum, hydrangeas, dahlias, geraniums, wild grasses, bachelor's buttons, cleomes, gladiolus, and corn cockle are among the many shrubs, trees, and flowers in season during summer. In fall, bouquet candidates to add to late-flowering sunflowers, coreopsis, and zinnias include Peruvian lilies, pomegranates, and persimmons on branches.

In this bouquet, 'Teddy Bear' and 'Autumn Beauty' sunflowers are combined with 'Medallion' and 'Bonica' roses.

late July, and in colder areas after all danger of frost has passed. Since most sunflower varieties require between sixty and eighty days to bloom, the last planting time should allow them to produce flowers before the first fall frosts.

Keep the ground moist until the seeds germinate. Thereafter, maintain adequate water in the root zone. Sunflowers may be affected by pests and disease, particularly aphids. Stem rot is a problem where there are hot wet summers, and in those areas plants should be spaced well apart to allow for maximum air circulation.

The flowers are best cut for bouquets when they are about three-quarters open, and the blooms will last up to a week if kept in water or slightly longer in floral preservative. The foliage does not last as long as the flower; it may begin to look limp and dry after two or three days and should be removed.

To grow sunflowers in containers, choose dwarf varieties and containers that are at least eighteen inches deep and twelve inches across. The seeding and maintenance instructions are the same as those for garden-planted sunflowers, but dilute liquid fertilizer will be needed every week once the first leaves have appeared.

Sunflowers can be started inside in small pots or other containers and then later transplanted outside. Germinating sunflower seeds in cut-off milk or juice cartons is an instructive project to do with children, as growth occurs quickly and can be observed daily close at hand. The watching child is rewarded with early success because the first leaves emerge in only a few days. Once the sunflowers have four to six leaves, transplant them to a larger container outside or directly into the garden.

SAVING SUNFLOWER SEEDS

If you forgo cutting a few blooms for bouquets, you can harvest seeds to sow next season. Seeds from hybrids will not grow true to type, however, and only the seeds of the open-pollinated should be saved for planting. Sunflower seeds can be harvested when the head is so dry that the seeds can be rubbed out readily. If the seeds are fully formed in the head but you are in a humid or cool climate where the heads won't dry fully outside, or it is already near the end of the season, cut off the head and dry it inside until the seeds are hard and can be rubbed out. Leave the loose seeds out to dry until they are no longer spongy when they are squeezed. If they are stored while they still have discernible moisture, they will heat and become moldy. Remove all broken seeds and bits of the head. Sunflower seeds have a relatively high oil content, so broken or cracked seeds will turn rancid. Store only sound seeds in somewhat airtight cans or plastic bags in a cool, dry place well protected from rodents, which have an affinity for them. It is advisable to add a few mothballs since there are undoubtedly some weevil eggs in with the seeds.

There are many, many varieties of sunflower, with new introductions by seed companies every year. Here are some used in the cut-flower trade that are especially successful, and although there are perennial varieties as well, these are all annuals. I like to grow several different varieties each year, always classic golds with chocolate centers, and a mixture of other shades.

BRANCHING

Evening Sun (*Helianthus annuus*) comes in a truly spectacular and varied palette of colors. Flowers of rusty red, chocolate brown, some with concentric rings of dusty gold, yellow, or even pinkish tones, are dominant. The foliage is dark blue-green with tinges of maroon on the edges, and the fine hairs on the stems are maroon as well. The flowers range in size from eight inches across for the central bloom to the more typical four to five inches across on the side-shoot blooms. The medium-sized centers are deep brown. Several plants will produce hundreds of blossoms over the season, and the stalks themselves grow to over seven feet. If you prefer continuous bloom without the height, plant in successive seedings and remove the mature plants as they become too large.

Autumn Beauty (*H. annuus*) bears flowers similar in size and color to those of 'Evening Sun,' but the majority are in golds and browns, with fewer of the rust and reddish shades. The foliage is dark green with a slight maroon cast, but to a lesser degree than that of 'Evening Sun.' The plant grows to a height of seven feet.

Red Sun (*H. annuus*), as might be expected from the name, has reddish flowers, although often tinged yellow-orange near the dark brown center and on the petal tips. The foliage is bright green tinged with maroon, a color that is especially evident on newly formed buds. Flowers from eight inches across form on the central stems, and from three to four inches across on the side shoots. The plant grows to six feet.

Vanilla Ice (*H. debilis*) has pale, creamy small flowers, generally no larger than four inches across, with small, black button centers. The central stalk, which is not particularly significant, has an open growth habit sporting apple green foliage.

NONBRANCHING

Sunbeam *(H. annuus)* is a hybrid, nonshedding variety with large flowers up to ten inches in diameter, of deep gold with golden green centers. The foliage is bright green, and the plants have a strong central stalk that grows to approximately five feet.

Sunbright *(H. annuus)* is a hybrid, nonshedding variety similar in size, color, and growth habit to 'Sunbeam,' but the centers of the flowers are dark brown.

Sunrich Lemon *(H. annuus)* and **Sunrich Orange** *(H. annuus)*, like the preceding varieties, are hybrids, but they are larger plants, growing to six feet or more. The flowers are from eight to ten inches across with dark brown centers, and are bright yellow and orange, respectively.

Sungold *(H. annuus),* which exists in both a standard and a dwarf form, is a most unusual looking sunflower because no center disk is visible and the petals are tightly packed in chrysanthemumlike layers. Fluffy, yellow-gold flowers on both types are about six inches in diameter on thick stalks, surrounded by very thick, large, bright green leaves packed tightly the length of the stalk. The dwarf variety, which is sometimes called 'Teddy Bear,' grows to only two feet and is a good container choice. The standard reaches to about five feet.

Big Smile *(H. annuus)* is a dwarf variety sporting yellow flowers with nearly black centers. The flowers may be up to eight inches across, growing on stalks of no more than one and one-half feet with bright green foliage. Like dwarf 'Sungold,' this is a good choice for container plantings.

OVERWATERING SUNFLOWERS

If the ground becomes soupy, the roots of tall, mature sunflowers with heavy heads and thick stalks will lose their grip, and topple. More than once I have forgotten a running hose in a sprinkler overnight and have been dismayed to see my sunflowers leaning precariously the next morning. If this happens, let the ground dry a bit, then pull them upright, packing the soil back around their bases to support them.

ZINNIA

Of summer's palette of flowers, zinnias are among the brightest and most varied. They exist in every color except blue, including a green one called 'Envy,' and show up variegated and two-toned as well. Tiny 'Lilliput,' a scant ten inches tall, can easily be grown in containers, but so can the three-foot-high 'State Fair.' Shapes vary from domelike beehives, a towering stack of florets and petals, to the pointed and rolled petals of the cactus types. All of their blooms are easily integrated into mixed bouquets, but they are also perfectly satisfying on their own. The small-headed blossoms are ideal for tabletop arrangements, while the larger ones become statuesque in a tall container.

Prolific and quick to grow in the warming days of late spring and early summer, zinnia plants will continue to flourish and to produce blooms until the first freezes of fall. Even the seed heads are attractive; as the flower matures, the colorful outer petals begin to fall away from the growing seed head, which is increasingly covered with the tiny yellow blooms of the florets, making colorful domes. I often include these in fresh bouquets, or dry them to use in dried-flower arrangements in winter.

Zinnias perform the best in a warm, dry setting. In warm but wet or damp conditions, established zinnias are beset by powdery mildew, making for scruffy foliage. In this case, successive plantings every two weeks will give you fresh, young plants to cut from, or you can choose from among the mildew-resistant varieties. In all cases, cutting encourages repeated blooming.

Zinnia seeds are medium-sized, narrow, and so light you can barely feel them in your hand, and they can scatter in the wind as you try to plant them. Select a sunny planting location, one that receives at least three-quarters to a full day of sun. These are heat-loving plants and will not perform well in cool, shady plots. Plant the seeds of all varieties about one-quarter inch deep, with spacing depending upon the eventual size of the plant. Sow dwarf varieties one and one-half to two inches apart, and the larger varieties up to a foot apart from midspring through midsummer in areas with a

DRYING ZINNIAS

When the flowers are fully open, up to when three-quarters of their petals are gone, cut the zinnias on long stems and strip off their leaves. Lay the flowers on a flat, newspaper-covered surface in a warm, dry location, preferably with circulating air, and out of direct sunlight. A ventilated attic or a garage is a good choice. To dry them upright, place a wire-mesh screen across an empty bucket and slip the stems through the holes to hold the flowers in a natural position. In one to two weeks, depending upon the climate, the flowers will be dry. Pack them loosely between sheets of newspaper in a box and store the box in a dry place until needed. They make exquisite elements in dried wreaths, especially in combination with soft tones such as that of sage.

FLORAL PRESERVATIVES

Floral preservatives, either in liquid or powdered form, are mixtures of chemicals that when added to water preserve the quality and life of cut flowers. Whenever possible, preservatives should be used in both the conditioning and the vase water. Preservatives are composed of three main ingredients: sugars, germicides, and acidifiers. The sugar feeds the flowers, providing the energy needed for the flower to continue to grow and open its buds. Germicides kill the microorganisms such as bacteria, fungi, molds, and yeasts that grow in the vase and not only produce unpleasant odors and slime but also can clog the vascular tissues, preventing the upward passage of nutrients. Acidifiers lower the pH of the solution so that water and nutrients can more easily move up the flowers' stems.

Homemade preservatives can be used as well as commercial ones. Carbonated lemon-lime soft drinks, any nondiet brand, can be used to provide sugar to feed the flowers and citric acid to lower the pH. Chlorine bleach can be added in small quantities as a germicide. If you use these, dilute 12 ounces of lemon-lime drink and 1 tablespoon of chlorine bleach with 1 gallon of water.

mild winter climate, and elsewhere once the soil has warmed and there is no danger of frost, typically in May. Many of the zinnia varieties flower in only sixty days, so calculate the last planting time to allow blooming before the first fall frosts.

Keep the ground moist until the seeds germinate. Thereafter, maintain water in the root zone, preferably by watering at the base rather than using overhead sprinklers, in order to diminish the possibility of powdery mildew. Pests that attack zinnias include Japanese beetles and aphids. Harvest when the flowers are fully open. They will last up to six days in water, or as long as ten days with a floral preservative.

Any of the zinnia varieties may be grown in containers, but the large types, those growing to two feet or more, should be planted in a container at least eighteen inches deep and one foot across. The dwarf varieties can be successfully planted in more shallow containers, although eight inches deep is the minimum. The seeding and maintenance instructions are the same as those for garden-planted zinnias, but dilute liquid fertilizer will be needed on a weekly basis after the first two leaves appear.

Zinnias can be started inside in flats or small pots and then later planted outside, either directly in the ground or in containers.

Numerous varieties exist and, as with sunflowers, new ones are often introduced by seed companies. Flower types are classified by petals. Double-petaled flowers and semidouble flowers differ in that the center of the flower is visible in the semidoubled, but hidden from view in the doubled. Flat petals indicate little or no curling under the petal edges, whereas in the cactus types, the petal edges roll under and twist. Beehive zinnias form compact rounded heads made of flat petals and double flowers. Here is a selection of varieties among the types and sizes.

TALL

Ruffles (*Zinnia elegans*), a mildew-resistant hybrid, is one of the preferred varieties in the cut-flower trade. It has big, double and semidouble flowers that are three to three and one-half inches across on individual stems over two feet long. They come in bright shades of red, rose, and yellow.

Sunshine (*Z. elegans*), like 'Ruffles,' is a mildew-resistant hybrid with large, double-flowered, flat-petaled blooms, sometimes as much as four inches across on plants two and one-half to three feet tall. Bright reds, oranges, yellows, and cream are dominant colors.

California Giants (*Z. elegans*) is my favorite variety, and I always plant a lot of the flat-petaled, semidoubled flowers. The blooms are huge, sometimes as much as five inches across, and the plants themselves often reach nearly four feet. The colors include purple, pink, and cream, as well as bright reds, yellows, and oranges.

Cactus Flowered Bright Jewels (*Z. elegans*) runs a close second to 'California Giants' in my garden. The flowers, with their twisting, curling petals, are nearly as large, often more than four inches across, and grow on plants that are only slightly shorter than those of 'California Giants.' The color range includes shades of pale lavender and white, as well as purple, rose, and scarlet.

Envy (*Z. elegans*) is an unusual chartreuse and not to everyone's taste, but I like to use it in bouquet combinations with lots of white, cream, and green foliage. It is a flat-petaled, semidouble type, growing on two-foot-tall plants.

Pumila (*Z. elegans*) is often called 'Cut and Come Again,' although other zinnias have the same habit. It has flowers from two and one-half to three inches wide, flat petaled, and double and semidouble growing on plants two feet tall. Colors include shades of red, pink, rose, orange, yellow, and white.

SHORT

Lilliput (*Z. elegans*) produces small, beehive-shaped blooms, each one to one and one-half inches in diameter on plants only a foot and a half tall. The flowers are fully double in both bright and pastel colors.

Persian Carpet (*Z. haageana*) produces unusual double to semidouble blooms in reds, golds, and white, with varying shades of those colors splashed across the tips of the pointed petals. The flowers are approximately two inches across growing on one-foot-high plants.

COSMOS

Their finely cut foliage and shiny, round buds ensure that cosmos provide a great deal of textural variation even in unmixed bouquets. The tall plants grow to over four feet with petals in rose, pink, magenta, lavender, and white surrounding a bright yellow center. The few dwarf types display the same color range, but the plants grow to between twelve and twenty inches tall. Several varieties are bicolored, with the secondary hue tinting the inner or outer edges of the petals. Cosmos are for the most part flowers of slightly overlapping single petals framing bright yellow centers. One variety, 'Seashell,' has unusual tubular petals that look like shooting stars circling the center.

Although the prolific cosmos may bloom later than sunflowers and zinnias, they too are reliable bloomers until struck down by the first frosts. In my garden, I know when the soil is warm because the seeds dropped there by last year's cosmos start popping up around early May, about the same time the volunteer tomato seeds are appearing. Even in late fall, when the weather is still warm as it often is, cosmos seedlings spring up.

Cosmos can be grown virtually anywhere, and they need almost no care. It is, however, important to keep the flowers cut and remove any dead blooms, not only to ensure the continuing production of new flowers but also because bedraggled, ragtag plants with spent and drying blooms make it difficult to find and cut fresh blossoms.

The seeds look like little black dots and even one-quarter of an ounce contains nearly two thousand of them. Their tiny size makes it difficult to space them carefully, so consider overplanting them, then thinning the young plants to the desirable distance of nine to twelve inches apart. As with the other members of the sunflower family, cosmos needs a location with full sun or a minimum of three-quarters of a day of full sun. Too little light will result in skimpy bloom. Plant the seeds only a scant one-quarter inch deep from April though July in mild winter climates, and in other areas when

the soil has warmed and there is no danger of frost. Keep the ground moist until the seeds germinate. Thereafter, maintain water in the root zone, but do not overwater. Overwatering is an enemy of cosmos, particularly in warm humid areas, and can contribute to root and stem rot. Watch out for aphids, Japanese beetles, and leaf hoppers, which are pests on your plants.

Cut the flowers when they are about three-quarters open. They will last four to five days in water, and up to six to seven days with a floral preservative. Single or multiple flower stems may be harvested.

Cosmos may be started inside and then later transplanted outside, so if you have a short growing season, consider this option. Only the dwarf varieties are suitable for container planting, as the others develop deep, spreading roots. Containers must be at least eighteen inches deep and twelve inches across. The seeding and maintenance instructions are the same as for garden-planted cosmos, but dilute liquid fertilizer must be added on a weekly basis after the first two leaves appear.

New cosmos varieties are introduced frequently. Here is a sampling of some of the most handsome, both tall and dwarf.

TALL

Versailles Blush Pink
(Cosmos bipinnatus) is a tetraploid that bears extra-large blooms a full three inches across in clusters that rise on long stems above the plant's foliage, forming a crown of flowers. The colors are shades of pale pink or white, and some of the inner bases of the petals display a darker pink. The plants grow to four feet tall.

Versailles Tetra
(C. bipinnatus) has the same growth habit as 'Versailles Blush Pink,' with four-inch-wide flowers in brilliant rose-pink. The petal bases circling the bright yellow centers are dark crimson.

Sensation strain
(C. bipinnatus) is a standard early bloomer. The flowers, each about three inches across, bloom among the foliage of plants that reach four and one-half feet tall. Mixed colors include lilac, magenta, pink, and white. Separate white, 'Purity,' and separate crimson-rose, 'Dazzler,' are also available.

Seashell *(C. bipinnatus)* has fascinating petals that resemble rolled tubes in shades of rose, pink, and white. The flowers are about three inches across and bloom on plants that reach a height of four feet.

Psyche *(C. bipinnatus)* is unusual among the cosmos because it has a second, smaller inner ring of petals, making for a nearly double flower. The petal edges are wavy and slightly irregular. The plants grow to four feet and the flowers are three and a half inches across.

DWARF

Sonata *(C. bipinnatus),* with two- to three-inch flowers on plants only eighteen to twenty inches tall, is available as 'Sonata Fairy Mix' in pink, lilac, and rose, and in separate colors of white, pink, and carmine.

Sunny Red and **Sunny Gold** *(C. sulphureus)* have bright red and bright golden yellow flowers, respectively. Plant size is quite small, only twelve to eighteen inches high. The foliage is thicker than that of *C. bipinnatus,* and the stems are stiffer and somewhat waxy, as are the buds, which are as attractive as the flowers.

CONDITIONING FLOWERS

Once flowers have been cut, it is important that they are conditioned before being arranged. As soon as possible after cutting, place the cut flowers in a container of water to which a floral preservative has been added (see page 30, Floral Preservatives). Let the flowers stand at least two hours and up to twenty-four to allow them to be fully hydrated and in their best possible condition before being arranged.

Flowers or shrubs with woody stems, such as lilacs, should first have the tips of their stems slightly crushed before conditioning to allow them to draw up the water better. Also, daffodils should not be mixed with other flowers during conditioning, but conditioned on their own (see pages 128–129).

COREOPSIS

The flowers of coreopsis come in singles and doubles in shades of gold, yellow, mahogany, red, and rust on long stems that rise above the bright green foliage at the base of the plants. The round, waxy flower buds, especially those of the mahogany-colored *tinctoria*, are extremely attractive and add texture and interest to bouquets. Blooms start to appear in late spring and will continue until the onset of fall frosts. One caution, though: if the spent flowers are not removed, the plants will soon become scruffy, and it will be difficult to sort through to cut attractive blooms.

Both dwarf and tall coreopsis varieties are available, one an annual that will bloom from seed within several months, and several perennial types, which if planted from seed may not bloom until the following year. It is possible, however, to purchase the perennials as plants in spring that will flower that summer.

The seed size of the annual variety is similar to that of cosmos, making them difficult to space evenly, so consider overplanting and then thinning the young plants to a desirable distance of nine to twelve inches apart for the tall variety, three to four inches apart for the dwarfs. The perennial varieties have larger seeds and need not be overplanted. A location with full sun or at least three-quarters of a day of full sun is needed. Plant the seeds only a bare one-quarter inch deep. They may be sown from April through July where winters are mild, and in other areas once the soil has warmed and there is no danger of frost, typically late spring through early summer. Keep the ground moist until the seeds germinate. Thereafter, maintain water in the root zone. Happily, coreopsis are virtually pest and disease free. Fertilize the annual variety once, when the seedlings have six to eight true leaves. Perennials should be fertilized every year in spring or early summer when they put forth their leaves.

Harvest coreopsis when the flowers are nearly fully open. The cut flowers, either single stems or multiple branches, will last six to eight days in water, slightly longer in floral preservative.

Coreopsis may be started inside in flats or small pots and then later planted outside either directly in the ground or in containers. For container plantings, choose dwarf varieties and containers at least eighteen inches deep and twelve inches across. The seeding and maintenance instructions are the same as for garden-planted coreopsis.

GLASS FLORAL MARBLES

The marbles, when placed in a layer two to three inches deep in the bottom of a container, will hold the stems of flowers in place. If the flowers are large and heavy, such as sunflowers, a deeper layer will be needed. Once the flowers are arranged, add water.

TALL

Coreopsis tinctoria *(Coreopsis tinctoria)* is the annual variety. It has mahogany red flowers, some gold, and some gold tinged with the red. Multibranching and with a profusion of tight little red buds, the flower petals look like soft velvet when they first open. The plants grow to about two and half feet.

Mayfield Giants *(C. lanceolata)* produces single-petaled, bright yellow flowers on plants that reach over three feet.

Sunburst *(C. lanceolata)* has golden yellow, semidouble blossoms up to three inches across on rather long stems. The plant itself reaches a height of two and one-half to three feet.

DWARF

Coreopsis tinctoria *(C. tinctoria)* exists in a dwarf version as well, and exhibits the same branching, open-growth habit as its nondwarf namesake. The dwarf variety grows to only one and a half feet.

Baby Sun *(C. grandiflora)* has single blossoms with brown centers and bright gold flowers. Less branching and open than the tall varieties and the dwarf *Coreopsis tinctoria*, it has a compact growth habit. The plant reaches a height of about one and a half feet.

PINCUSHION FLOWER

It has even become somewhat difficult to get the seeds for pincushion flowers, truly old-time favorites that were once in everyone's summer garden bouquets. They are sometimes called sweet scabiosas because of their light fragrance, and the pointed, dome-shaped heads, composed of hundreds of tiny, fluffy florets, rest on long, strong, stiff stems that rise up and out of the dark green foliage of the plant, making for easy cutting. The colors are among my garden favorites: deep maroon, lavender, purplish rose, dark blue, salmon pink, and scarlet. The maroon is an unusual color and makes a striking bouquet on its own, in combination with bright yellows or oranges, or with flowers of a softer palette of pinks and mauves.

Although there are both annual and perennial varieties of *scabiosas*, only the easy-to-grow annual varieties, the pincushion flowers, are presented here. They are strong and steady bloomers from early summer until fall, with the longer stems being produced in midsummer. It is curious to watch the first flowers of the season develop. At first it seems as if no buds exist at all on the bushy plants, then gradually a tight dot reveals itself among the greens. As it slowly rises out of the foliage, the single dot begins to appear as many miniscule ones, with color beginning to show, surrounded by a ring of green. As the days go by, the buds take on the characteristic pyramid shape of the pincushion flower, and the lower ring of dots opens into individual florets. Each day more and more buds open until finally the full-blown flower rises erect on strong stems, ready to cut. But once the bloom has finished, the flower heads are a sorry sight, dryish brown and hairy looking, and are best kept snipped off.

Pincushion flowers have seeds that look like little sticks, but they are easy to handle. They need to be planted in a location with full sun. Even three-quarters of a day of full sun isn't enough to produce fully flowering plants. Since the germination of the seeds is enhanced by light, barely cover them with soil. Overplant the seeds and then thin the young plants to between nine and twelve inches apart. In areas with mild winter climates, sow the seeds from March through June or in fall for late-spring bloom. In other areas, plant them when the soil has warmed and there is no longer any danger of frost. Keep the ground moist until the seeds germinate. Thereafter, maintain water in the root zone. Fertilize when there are four to six true leaves.

Pincushion flowers are virtually disease and pest free, but their brittle stalks can be snapped by strong winds and may need staking. They may also be started inside in flats or small pots and then later planted into the ground. They are not particularly suitable for container planting.

Cut individual stems when the flowers are fully open. Once cut, they will last up to a week in water, and several days longer with the addition of floral preservatives.

Only a few selected varieties of the annual pincushion flower are available, compared to the large numbers one can find of sunflower and cosmos, and all are tall.

Imperial Mix
(Scabiosa atropurpurea) provides color combinations of deep maroon, rose, pink, lavender, and white. The plants reach three feet and have flowers one to one and a half inches in diameter on long stems.

Giant Double Mix
(S. atropurpurea) is a similar mix of large flowered types, although many grow to four feet tall.

QIS Dark Blue, QIS Salmon-Pink, and **QIS Scarlet**
(all *S. atropurpurea*) are single color selections developed in Holland especially for commercial cut-flower growers. The flowers are up to two inches across and have very long stems on plants growing to three feet tall.

Airy Fillers

Queen Anne's Lace and Bishop's Flower, Bachelor's Button,
Nigella, Sweet Sultan, Blue Lace Flower, and Cleome

Airy Fillers

A NUMBER OF FLOWERS HAVE LACY FOLIAGE, LACY FLOWER HEADS, OR BOTH, MAKING them ideal to fluff out bouquets and give them an airy yet full appearance. Cleome, nigella, bachelor's button, sweet sultan, blue lace flower, and Queen Anne's lace all fit this category. Adding several stems of fluffy, white Queen Anne's lace or a cutting of delicate pale blue nigella can turn three or four of summer's garden roses into a lush, replete bouquet. Sunflowers, zinnias, and pincushion flowers, in season along with the airy flowers, can be mixed together to create wild, exuberant expressions of summer in shades of bright orange, purple, red, and yellow, then filled in with the lighter pastels of the airy flowers and punctuated by deep blue bachelor's buttons.

Valued for their versatility in bouquet making, the airy flowers were especially popular during the nineteenth century when they were found in the cutting gardens of people of modest means, as well as in the elaborate estate gardens of the aristocracy. Cleomes (also called spider flowers), bachelor's buttons, and sweet sultans were important elements in Victorian gardens, figuring large in the classic nineteenth-century island garden of Celia Thaxter off the coast of Maine, so beautifully depicted by American impressionist Childe Hassam. Although the bachelor's button and Queen Anne's lace are still common garden elements today, cleomes, sweet sultans, and nigellas are near-forgotten. They are quick and easy to grow, however, and long lasting in the garden and in vases.

Once planted into warm garden soil and supplied with adequate moisture, green shoots of all but the blue lace flower, which may require as long as three weeks, will appear in seven to ten days, requiring only slightly longer than zinnias and sunflowers. When established and blooming, though, they require little further care than regular watering.

QUEEN ANNE'S LACE AND BISHOP'S FLOWER

Queen Anne's lace and the very similar bishop's flower are among the most popular filler flowers because their flower heads sometimes reach ten inches in diameter and are commonly at least eight inches. The large sprays of small white flowers and minute green buds make soft, muted colorings that blend well with flowers and foliages of all kinds. The stems are long, often up to four feet, and may develop curves and twists that add further interest to bouquets.

True Queen Anne's lace is the flowering seed head of the common carrot, *Daucus carota,* which doesn't flower until the second year after planting. But the garden-cultivated Queen Anne's lace, also called bishop's flower, white lace flower, and false Queen Anne's lace, is *Ammi majus,* a quick and easy-to-grow annual and the one whose cultivation is discussed here, as it is the one primarily grown for cut flowers. *D. carota* has a thicker, denser flower head than that of *A. majus,* and may become invasive.

Bishop's flower thrives in a warm, sunny setting, but can also take some shade. Unfortunately, it is subject to powdery mildew that discolors the foliage, but if this is a problem in your area, successive sowings will provide fresh-looking flowers and foliage from late spring through early fall.

Seeds are tiny, with fifty-four thousand of them in a single ounce, a quantity too small to fill the palm of your hand. Because of their size, they are nigh impossible to plant singly, and instead may be scatter-planted and then thinned to one foot apart. Sow them in early spring, and in fall as well in areas with mild winter climates. Keep the ground moist until the seeds germinate, which requires seven to fourteen days. Thereafter, maintain water in the root zone, preferably by watering at the base, as overhead sprinkling encourages mildew. The plants are large, with spreading branches and stems, and will require support to protect them from being blown over by winds or storms. Bishop's flower easily reseeds itself, and fall rains bring dozens of little seedlings in the garden where the seeds fell in summer.

Since the airy flowers bloom
from late spring into fall,
they are available as fillers
for the gamut of spring,
summer, and fall shrubs,
trees, grasses, and flowers.
They can be combined first in
late spring and early summer
with fruit blossoms on
branches, late tulips and
daffodils, sweet peas, roses,
lilacs, green nuts on branches,
and wildflowers. Then,
throughout the summer, they
can be grouped with roses,
larkspurs, hydrangeas,
sunflowers, zinnias,
pincushion flowers, dahlias,
lilies, and fruits. Later, as
fall approaches, grapes on
the vine, figs, and other late
fruits, plus fall-flowering
bulbs and early rosehips,
are suitable companions.

Here, a few stems of
'California Giant' zinnias in
red and yellow are combined
with sprays of Ammi majus
to make a summer bouquet.

FLORAL FOAM

Frequently referred to by the brand name Oasis, floral foam is a light green, firm, spongelike material that absorbs water. To use it, first cut it with a sharp knife into a size to suit the container. Then soak the foam in water until bubbles stop rising and it has become heavy with moisture. Place the soaked foam in the container, and stick the flower stems into it until the blooms are arranged to your satisfaction. Finally, fill the container with water.

My first experience with floral foam was disastrous. I placed the unsoaked foam in the bottom of a vase, stuck flowers into it, and filled the vase with water. The foam immediately floated to the top, tumbling the flowers.

Floral foam comes in a wide variety of shapes and sizes, including blocks, cones, circles, balls, and nosegays. Some are encased in plastic mesh for ease of use.

Cut bishop's flowers when the outer flowers are opened, but the inner ones are still in bud. Gloves are recommended when harvesting because the sticky sap that exudes from the stem can cause skin reactions.

The seeds can be started inside in flats or small pots, but sowing them directly in the garden is recommended, as alternating temperatures are required for the best germination. Alternating temperatures occur naturally outside, but indoors they must be simulated.

These flowers are not suitable for container planting because of their deep roots and considerable height.

Seed for bishop's flower is commonly sold labeled as white lace flower or simply by its Latin name, *Ammi majus.* Two named varieties are also available.

White lace flower *(Ammi majus)* has white flowers on a spreading head of four to six inches. It grows to about four feet, and support is optional.

Snowflake *(A. majus)* has white flowers on a spreading flower head of up to ten inches, although more commonly six to eight inches. It grows to between three feet and five feet tall. It is best to provide support for the plant.

Silverdill *(A. majus)* is similar to 'Snowflake,' but it has a slight green tinge.

BACHELOR'S BUTTON

Almost as appealing in a bouquet as the blue, wine, rose, and white blossoms of bachelor's buttons are their strapping gray-green foliage and tiny gray-green buds, the color of which blends well with other greens and with virtually any hue. Bachelor's buttons vary in size from dwarfs suitable for container plantings to varieties nearly three feet tall. Most have double flowers and will bloom from early summer through fall. If the dead flowers are not removed, however, the plants will begin to look shabby and the bloom will diminish.

Like most of the summer annuals, also called cornflowers, bachelor's buttons perform best in a warm, dry setting where they can receive adequate water. In very warm, humid settings, the plants can develop powdery mildew.

The thin needle-shaped seeds are about one-half inch long and are so light and fluffy that a pillowcase full of them weighs only a few pounds. On a windy day they are apt to fly out of your hand as you plant them.

Choose a sunny planting location that receives at least three-quarters of a day of full sun, although in hot climates bachelor's buttons can tolerate some shade. Sow the seeds about one-quarter inch deep, with dwarf varieties spaced about four inches apart and larger ones six to eight inches, from late spring through early summer in areas with mild winters, and in fall as well, for spring bloom. In other areas, they may be sown when the soil has warmed and there is no longer any danger of frost.

Keep the ground moist until the seeds germinate, usually seven to ten days. Thereafter, maintain adequate water in the root zone. Once the plants are mature, avoid using overhead sprinklers, as their force is enough to knock over the stems. Alternatively, provide the plants with support by loosely tying them to a stake.

Like cleomes and nigellas, bachelor's buttons are relatively free of disease and insect problems.

Harvest bachelor's buttons as soon as the flowers are open, either by single flower stem or by branches that include leaves and buds and many other flower stems. They will last four to five days in water, or up to seven or eight days with a floral preservative.

Although any of the bachelor's button varieties may be grown in containers, the dwarf types are particularly suitable. These grow to one and one-half feet and require little or no staking. The dwarfs may be planted in containers at least eight inches in diameter and eight inches deep, while the standard sizes should have containers at least ten inches deep and twelve inches in diameter. The seeding instructions and maintenance are the same as those for garden-planted bachelor's buttons, but the container plants will need to be fertilized weekly with a dilute liquid fertilizer.

Bachelor's buttons can be started inside in flats or small pots and then later planted outside, either directly in the ground or in containers.

A number of bachelor's buttons varieties are available, some in separate single colors, others in mixes. The tall varieties all have the open, branching habit characteristic of old-fashioned bachelor's buttons, and these are my preferences.

TALL

Emperor William (*Centaurea cyanus*) is an old-fashioned variety that grows to nearly three feet tall, with single-petaled, dark blue blossoms. It will require staking, or propping up by other flowers in the garden.

Blue Boy (*C. cyanus*) has clear, bright blue double blossoms on plants that grow to two feet. They may require staking.

Pinkie (*C. cyanus*) displays bright rose-pink double flowers upon opening that fade to pale pink as they age. The plants grow to between one and one-half to two feet tall.

Red Boy (*C. cyanus*) has deep, dark red—nearly maroon—double blossoms on plants that grow to between one and one-half to two feet tall.

Snowman (*C. cyanus*) is the compatriot of 'Pinkie,' but with bright, pure white double blossoms upon opening, although they dull thereafter.

DWARF

Baby Blue (*C. cyanus*) grows in a compact, ball-like shape reaching a height of only one foot when fully grown. The flowers are semidouble and bright blue.

Baby Pink (*C. cyanus*) grows in the same fashion as 'Baby Blue,' the only difference being the flowers are bright pink.

Polka Dot Mixed (*C. cyanus*) is a mixture of white, blue, red, and pink flowers growing in a branching form to about one foot.

Jubilee Gem (*C. cyanus*) has bright blue flowers growing on branching plants that reach about one foot.

NIGELLA

An herb of Mediterranean origin, nigella comes in various forms, but only three of them are typically cultivated for cut flowers: *Nigella damascena, N. hispanica,* and *N. orientalis.*

The first, and by far the best known, is frequently called by its common name, love-in-a-mist. It is a small plant, rarely growing to more than a foot and a half high even in the richest of soils, and it sports small, star-shaped flowers of blue, white, or pink surrounded by finely cut sprays of lacy green. It is this combination of foliage and flower that makes it such an excellent filler for small bouquets—even bridal bouquets. A clutch of only white nigella sprays, blossoms, and foliage interspersed with white roses makes a complete bouquet. The interesting seedpods, balloon-shaped with little curved tips, are green when immature, turning to dark magenta striped with deep green when mature, and these too are fine elements in both fresh and dried bouquets.

FROGS AND WIRE MESH

Flower frogs take many forms. Some are of glass, and others are of metal crisscrossed to form an arched grid. Still others, metal bases topped with tightly packed metal spikes, are sometimes called pinholders and the stems are thrust onto the spikes. Frogs were far more common twenty or thirty years ago than today, so good places to look for them are flea markets and collectible shops.

Wire mesh with medium- to large-sized holes can be cut with wire snips to fit inside your container. It can be domed or crumpled to create a frog that will hold flower stems.

N. hispanica has deep purple, wide blossoms larger than those of love-in-a-mist and, although the foliage is similar, lacy and full, the pod is quite different—elongated and with large, flaring tips. The pods, the flowers, and the foliage are coveted for bouquets. *N. orientalis* grows to nearly three feet and has large, golden yellow blossoms, the characteristic lacy foliage of the other nigellas, and seedpods similar to those of *N. hispanica.*

In the garden, nigella performs best in a warm to medium-warm setting where it can receive frequent waterings. Indicative of its wild origins, the hardy plant is rarely plagued by pests or disease.

The seeds are small, black, and quite shiny. Those of *N. hispanica* are much smaller than those of *N. damascena*, while those of *N. orientalis* are twice as large. Sow the seeds in an area that receives three-quarters to a full day of sun, although in areas with hot summers, they can be successfully grown in partial shade. Plant the seeds shallowly, only about one-quarter of an inch deep, and an inch or two apart from early spring into midsummer, and into fall in areas with mild winters. Keep moist until germination occurs, which is in seven to ten days. Nigella reseeds easily if the seedpods are allowed to burst and fall in the garden, so soon there will be a veritable blanket of the blossoms, even in colder areas. Once the seeds have germinated, keep the plants well watered throughout their period of bloom.

Harvest all of the nigella varieties as soon as the flowers begin to appear. They will last three to four days in water, or as long as five or six days with a floral preservative.

Any of the nigellas may be grown in containers at least twelve inches across and twelve inches deep, although dwarf nigella is especially suitable. The seeding and maintenance instructions are the same as for garden-planted nigellas, but weekly application of a dilute fertilizer is necessary. Nigellas do not transplant well and are best sown in place, directly in the garden or container.

A half dozen or so named varieties of cultivated nigellas exist, both mixed and in single colors.

SIMPLE STAKING METHODS

Insert several thin bamboo stakes around the edge of the plant, and loop string through them. Or drive a single, sturdy cane of bamboo or a stake into the ground next to a plant and loosely tie the plant to it, adding ties as the plant grows. This works best for plants with a single central stem or stalk.

Tall, bushy plants may need more support than either of these two methods can provide, however. In this case, insert a collection of leafless twigs into the ground to prop up the branches as the plant grows.

As you observe the plant's growth habit, it will become apparent which support method is most appropriate. All of these staking methods are applicable to container plants as well.

DRYING THE PODS OF
LOVE-IN-A-MIST FOR ARRANGEMENTS

The dried purple balloonlike pods of this flower, surrounded by their spidery foliage, add unusual detail to arrangements, whether dried or in combination with fresh leaves on flowers. Leave the pods on the plant to develop their color fully. Once they are firm to the touch and their stripes have turned deep magenta, cut the stems at the base of the plant. Strip away all but the uppermost leaves, and hang the pod-topped stems upside down in a warm, dry location, or lay them on a flat, newspaper-covered surface in a similar environment. Once the pods are fully dried and the seeds inside rattle when shaken, pack them loosely between sheets of newspaper in a box and store the box in a dry place until needed. The pods of N. hispanica may be dried in the same way.

Miss Jekyll
(Nigella damascena), which grows to about one and one-half feet, is available in four colors, 'Deep Blue,' 'Rose,' 'Sky-Blue,' and 'White,' as well as in a mixture of those shades.

Persian Jewels
(N. damascena), a mixture of rose, pink, blue, and white flowers, is a little shorter than 'Miss Jekyll,' growing to slightly over a foot.

Shorty Blue *(N. damascena),* a dwarf variety with dark blue flowers, climbs to only ten inches.

Nigella hispanica
(N. hispanica) has deep purple blossoms and grows to approximately one and a half feet.

Transformer *(N. orientalis)* displays bright yellow flowers and grows to two feet or more.

SWEET SULTAN

Richly fragrant sweet sultan once had an important place in gardens and bouquets. It is in the same genus as the bachelor's button, and they resemble each other in the minaret shape of the buds and the color of their foliage. Sweet sultans, however, have succulent stems that are often two feet long and two inches wide; fluffy blossoms in pale shades of mauve, cream, rose and soft yellow; and deeply serrated leaves, unlike the thin and strappy foliage of the bachelor's button.

Sweet sultan is quick to grow, and seeds sown in spring are likely to produce flowers within two months. Nearly free of pests and diseases, the plants are prolific producers of blossoms from spring throughout summer, even when grown in poor soil.

The seeds are light and smooth to the touch. They should be planted in a sunny location that receives at least three-quarters to a full day of sun, and sown one-quarter inch deep and five to six inches apart. Later the seedlings should be thinned to a foot apart, as the plants become quite large and branching. Seeds may be sown from midspring through early summer where winters are mild, and in other areas once the soil has warmed and all danger of frost has passed.

Keep the ground moist until the seeds germinate, about ten days from sowing, and then maintain water in the root zone. To reduce the possibility of powdery mildew, water the plants at the base rather than with overhead sprinklers.

Cut the flowers when they are brightly colored and fully open. They may also be harvested in bud form. Once cut, they will last three to four days in water, or up to five to six days with a floral preservative.

The seeds may also be started inside in flats or small pots and then later planted outside, either directly in the ground or in containers. Seeding instructions are the same as those for garden-planted sweet sultans. Because of their size and thick root, sweet sultans need a container at least two feet deep and a foot across.

Although single-colored varieties of sweet sultans are available, primarily in Europe, the seeds most commonly found here are a mixture of all the colors.

Imperialis *(Centaurea moschata)* includes white, lavender, pink, and deep purple flowers. The branching plants grow to two and one-half feet.

The Bride *(C. moschata)* bears bright white flowers on branching plants that reach about two feet.

BLUE LACE FLOWER

ozens of tiny blue florets make up the three-inch-wide lavender-blue flower heads that sit atop long stems rising out of lacy, dark green foliage. Of all of the filler flowers, blue lace is the only one that prefers cool climates and cool weather. In my hot summer climate, it stops blooming in early June, just as the other airy flowers are beginning, but in cooler coastal areas it continues to bloom throughout the summer, producing an abundance of flowers for cutting.

Pale brown, dry, and narrow, the tiny seeds resemble those of dill. They should be sown in a sunny location that has at least three-quarters of a day of full sun, preferably in a lighter soil that drains well. Sow the seeds in late spring about one-half inch deep and three inches apart, then thin to ten inches apart. Keep the ground moist until the seeds germinate, which may take up to twenty days. Once germinated, maintain water in the root zone.

Cut blue lace flowers for bouquets when the outer florets have opened but the inner ones are still in bud. The flowers will last four to five days in water, the inner florets slowly opening, and up to eight days with a floral preservative.

Blue lace flower is suitable for growing in a container if the container is large enough to accom-modate the root system and the size of the plant, usually about two feet deep and one foot across. Seeding and maintenance instructions are the same as for in the garden, but the plants will need to be fertilized weekly with a dilute fertilizer. They often do not take well to transplanting, so it is preferable to start them directly in the garden or container.

There are only two varieties of blue lace flowers available.

Blue lace flower
(Trachymene coerulea, formerly *Didiscus coeruleus)* has lavender-blue blossoms two to three inches wide on branching plants between two and three feet tall.

Madonna *(T. coerulea)* is a recently developed variety that has white flowers tinged with lavender.

CLEOME

Also called spider flower because of its spider-leg-like stamens and pistils, the cleome is a highly underrated cut flower. Its flower heads, reaching eight inches in diameter, are a combination of dozens of small flowers with long, spidery stamens and pistils, tubular buds, and long, thin, arching seedpods. The seedpods remain pale green until the last of the flowers on the head have bloomed, which make take a week or more. Because of the unusual character of the flower head, the long stems (often two feet or more in length), and its long-lasting vase life, cleome deserves to reclaim its place as an important cut flower.

The blooms are of purest white, or shades of pink or violet, and the thorned and strongly scented plants themselves, with somewhat sticky, deeply lobed, bright green leaves, grow to nearly five feet. The more the flowers are cut, the taller the plant becomes, putting forth more and more flowers.

Cleome performs best in a warm, dry garden setting, and suffers little insect or disease problems. Although it will grow its largest and bloom more profusely when well watered, it is also considered a rather drought-tolerant plant, as it will grow and bloom even in poor soil once established.

The seeds are small, round, and black—similar to those of poppies, but larger—and are best planted in a sunny location that receives at least three-quarters of a day of full sun. Plant the seeds about one-quarter inch deep, and space them six inches apart. Eventually the seedlings should be thinned to one foot apart, as the plants are wide as well as tall, branching to a diameter of three feet and, by fall, well over five feet in height.

In areas with mild winter climates, sow the seeds from midspring through midsummer. They often will reseed themselves. In colder climates, plant in spring after danger of frost has passed, as the cleome has little resistance and is quickly damaged. Keep the ground moist until germination occurs, generally in about ten days. Thereafter, maintain water in the root zone.

The flower head blooms in layers, or circlets, with the lower flowers showing first. Flowers may be cut for bouquets when several circlets of blossoms have opened, or later when the first circlets have flowered and left behind developing seedpods and the upper blooms are open. In the latter case, remove the dead blossoms and leave the seedpods. Once cut, the flowers will last three to four days in water, or up to five to six days with a floral preservative.

Cleome is not suited to container plantings because of the very long, deep roots it develops, although it can be started inside in flats or small pots and then later planted outside. In areas with late frost, this is the preferred procedure.

Varieties of cleome are available in separate colors or mixed, or you can make a personal mixture by combining the seeds of single colors, 'Cherry Queen' and 'Violet Queen,' for example.

White Queen (*Cleome hasselerana*), also called 'Helen Campbell,' has bright, pure white flowers.

Cherry Queen (*C. hasselerana*) has vibrant cherry-colored buds that open to soft pink.

Violet Queen (*C. hasselerana*), my favorite, has reddish violet buds that open in the same shade, but paler.

Color Fountain (*C. hasselerana*) is a mixture of colors, including pink, rose, violet, and white.

Tamed from the Wild

Lupine and Poppy

Tamed from the Wild

LUPINES AND POPPIES, WHICH FLOURISH IN THE WILD, HAVE BEEN TAMED BY PLANT breeders, and certain strains have been selected and developed to perform well for home gardeners and for growers of cut flowers for the floral trade. From the sidewalk flower shops of Paris to the farmers' market stalls of California, one sees tall spires of Russell lupines and bunches of brilliant-hued Iceland and Shirley poppies standing in buckets of water, waiting to be taken home and plumped into vases.

When cut from the garden and gathered into bouquets, poppies and lupines bring a feeling of wildflower-blanketed meadows and hillsides indoors. The poppies will unfurl in their vases when cut on long stems, their buds just beginning to open as they lift up their gracefully bent necks. The upright stems of purple lupines or the gently bent ones of the tall, multicolored Russell lupines will slowly open their myriad buds in the warmth of the indoors.

In flower markets, though, one doesn't often find the multicolored California poppies or the French red poppies that are so easily available to the home gardener and which make such out-standing bouquet flowers. Here, the home gardener has the lead over commercial production. The bright orange poppy that carpets the springtime hills of California and the red poppy that appears en masse in the wheat fields and along the roadsides of France, Spain, and Italy were once the source of simple bouquets, gathered with the wild lupines that flower at the same season. Plant breeders now have created California poppies in bright red, cream, pink, and other variations, as well as the classic orange for garden-growing.

Both lupines and poppies prefer cool growing conditions, and either cease to bloom under summer's intense heat or produce only small, truncated flowers. Typically, they are planted in fall through early spring in mild winter climates, and in early spring elsewhere. In mild winter climates, however, the Iceland poppy blooms in winter and spring from fall transplants or summer-sown seed.

LUPINE

In spring, California's wild lupine turns roadsides to purple with its ten-inch spikes of small, white-throated purple flowers on plants a foot and a half high, while another species, the 'Texas Bluebonnet,' turns the Midwest plains blue. Occasionally one can spot a yellow spike or white spike. The wild strains perform well in garden soil, as do the hybrid Russell lupines that were developed for garden ornamentals and cut flowers.

Russell lupines, easy to grow perennials, produce two- to three-foot-long spikes of flowers set with hundreds of blossoms in red, rose, pink, yellow, salmon, or pale lavender for making long-lasting bouquets. Because of their height and heavy heads, they may need support in the garden to protect them from strong winds and driving rains. Lupines, like poppies, prefer cool weather, and will stop blooming and go to seed when the weather turns hot.

Plant seeds one-half inch deep and two inches apart in fall through early spring in areas with a mild winter climate, and elsewhere in early spring after the danger of frost has passed.

Keep the ground moist until the seeds germinate, which may take up to three weeks. Thereafter, maintain water in the root zone, preferably watering at the base of the Russell lupines rather than with overhead sprinklers, to avoid knocking down their long spikes. Lupines are relatively free from disease and pests.

Cut the wild strains when the lower blossoms of the spike have opened but the upper portion is still in bud. Cut the Russell lupine when the lower one-third has opened but the remaining buds are closed. Once placed indoors in water, the closed buds will open over several days. The cut flowers will last three to four days in water, or up to five to six days with a floral preservative.

Seeds are available for the wild lupine strains, as well as for the cut-flower hybrids.

*In spring and early summer
when poppies and lupines are
in bloom, so are sweet peas,
nasturtiums, wildflowers,
grasses, magnolias, flax,
tulips, daffodils, freesias,
larkspurs, early roses, lilacs,
hyacinths, lilies-of-the-valley,
wisteria, and peonies. Herbs
such as thyme are flowering,
and rosemary and sage are
showing new, fresh growth,
as is sweet bay laurel. Pear,
apple, quince, and peach
trees are blossoming, too.*

*Here, delicate Russell
lupine mixes with delphinium,
sweet peas, columbine, and
roses to create a spring
bouquet.*

Blue lupine
(Lupinus succulentus), a perennial in areas with mild winter climates, has bluish purple blossoms with a white or yellow throat and flat, splayed, multi-petaled leaves of dark blue-green. It grows between one and one and one-half feet tall.

Texas Bluebonnet *(L. texensis)* resembles *L. succulentus,* but the blossoms are somewhat smaller and more blue than purple.

Tall Russell Hybrids
(L. polyphyllus) are available in a wide range of colors, including 'Chandelier,' which is shades of yellow; 'The Pages,' in shades of deepest red, and 'Noble Maiden,' in pale cream to pure white. The leaves are like those of *L. succulentus,* splayed and deep blue-green. The plants grow to about three feet and will need support.

Dwarf Gallery Hybrids
(L. polyphyllus) are half the size of the 'Tall Russells,' growing to only a foot and a half. They are available in many shades. 'Gallery' mixture includes blues, pinks, reds, whites, yellows, and bicolors. The colors are also available singly: 'Gallery Blue,' 'Gallery Pink,' 'Gallery Red,' 'Gallery White,' and 'Gallery Yellow.'

POPPY

Although there are many types of poppies, I have chosen to include here only those annuals that are the easiest to grow, the California and the Shirley, as well as the Iceland, which, although it is a biennial, is treated as an annual in the garden.

The California poppy is not usually thought of as a long-lasting bouquet flower, but it and its lacy, sage-colored foliage will look fine for up to five days if cut just as the buds are unfolding. The flowers may be double or single in colors ranging from the bright scarlet of 'Dalli' to the tender lavender of 'Purple Gleam.' In between are all shades of orange, yellow, and cream. White is represented, and so are pink and rose. When the flower is spent, the long, thin, round, pointed pod begins to develop, which also can be attractive in bouquets when still green. Once dry, the pod will split open, releasing hundreds of seeds that, if given warmth and water, will readily reseed.

If cut just as the buds begin to open and put immediately into water, the Mediterranean's red corn poppy, also called the Flanders field poppy, will last for several days. The gardener can choose strains of this classic poppy, including the Shirley, in red, pink, or white; red with a black cross at the throat; or even soft gray or ivory. The plump buds, covered with soft hairs and hanging downward on graceful stems, and the seedpods that are round and green and tinged with black at their slightly ruffled top, make textural additions to bouquets. Like the California poppy, they will readily reseed themselves given a welcoming environment.

From the Iceland poppy, a wildflower in the Arctic regions, varied strains have been selected and developed by plant breeders to produce brilliant colors ranging from orange and yellow to deep salmon and pale pink. Its buds and long stems covered with fine black hairs are quite a bit larger than those of the Shirley poppies and make magnificent cut flowers. The big, green seedpods can be incorporated into bouquets as well. Plants that grow more than a foot and a half may need support and protection from wind.

California, Shirley, and Iceland poppies all thrive in a sunny location where they can receive adequate water. Few pests bother them, with the exception of whitefly, which may attack the Iceland poppy. Watering should be done at the base of the plants rather than with overhead sprinklers. This is especially true for the Iceland poppies, which are less sturdy than the California and the Shirley and are more easily damaged.

There are about six hundred fifty round, black seeds per gram of California poppy, so they are considerably larger than those of either the Iceland or the Shirley, which have over eight thousand seeds per gram. For easier handling, all three seeds may be mixed with sand and scattered over prepared ground, and then covered with one-quarter inch of soil and sprinkled. Keep the soil moist until the seeds germinate, which will take three to four weeks. Thereafter, keep moisture in the root zone. Keeping the poppies well watered extends their bloom considerably. In mild winter climates, sow the seed in fall, winter, or spring for spring and early summer bloom, and elsewhere sow in early spring for summer bloom.

Cut the poppies for bouquets when the buds are just starting to open. Place the cut stems in water, then singe them with a flame and replace them in water. The cut flowers will last three to four days in water, or five to six days with a floral preservative.

The poppies may be grown in containers at least ten inches deep and ten inches across. Follow the seeding and maintenance instructions for garden-planted poppies, but add a dilute liquid fertilizer weekly. The Iceland poppies can also be started inside in flats or small pots and then planted outside or in containers. Seedlings of Iceland poppies are commonly available in nurseries and garden centers and are good choices for transplanting either into containers or into the garden.

SINGEING POPPY STEMS

To ensure the longest vase life for poppies, have a bucket of water at your side in the garden. Gather only flowers that have just begun to open, and plunge the cut stem immediately into the water, then bring the flowers inside. Singe the tip of each stem with a flame, easily done by lighting a candle and putting the stem end in the fire for a few seconds. Return the flowers to the water.

Numerous varieties of California, Shirley, and Iceland poppies are available, with more being developed by breeders and offered by seed companies each year.

CALIFORNIA

Alba *(Eschscholzia californica)* has creamy white blossoms and grows to about one foot.

Purple Gleam *(E. californica)* has delicately shaded blossoms of mauve with slightly yellow throats on plants that reach to about one foot.

Red Chief *(E. californica)* sports scarlet blossoms on plants that grow to about one foot.

Golden West *(E. californica)*, the classic bright orange poppy of the California hillsides, grows to about one and one-half feet.

Dalli *(E. californica)* has bicolored blossoms in shades of red and yellow, which grow on a compact plant that reaches one foot.

Thai Silk *(E. californica)* has blossoms with slightly wavy edges in shades of bright pink, orange, yellow, and red. The plant grows to just under a foot.

Double Ballerina Mixed *(E. californica)* has unusual blossoms with fluted edges in varying shades of yellow, cream, orange, and pink on a plant that grows to about one foot.

SHIRLEY

Fairy Wings *(Papaver rhoeas)*, also called 'Mother of Pearl,' has unusual gray, pale blue, pale pink, and white blossoms two to three inches in diameter on plants about one and one-half feet tall.

Shirley Mixed *(P. rhoeas)* is the classic collection of old-fashioned blooms one and one-half to two inches in diameter in shades of white, red, and pink on plants that grow to between one and two feet tall.

American Legion *(P. rhoeas)* is bright red with black marks resembling a cross at the throat. The blossoms are larger than those of 'Shirley Mixed' and have a more crinkled, crepe-paper texture. Plants reach a height of between one and two feet.

ICELAND

Wonderland Mixed *(Papaver nudicaule)* has flowers up to four inches in diameter in shades of orange, yellow, and white on plants that grow to approximately one foot.

Oregon Rainbows *(P. nudicaule)* is a bright mixture of blossoms up to eight inches in diameter in shades of orange, salmon, cream, pink, and rose on plants up to two feet tall.

Champagne Bubbles *(P. nudicaule)* is a hybrid that bears large blooms, some over eight inches in diameter, in shades of light pink, white, and pale yellow on plants up to two feet tall.

Graceful Vines

Sweet Pea and Nasturtium

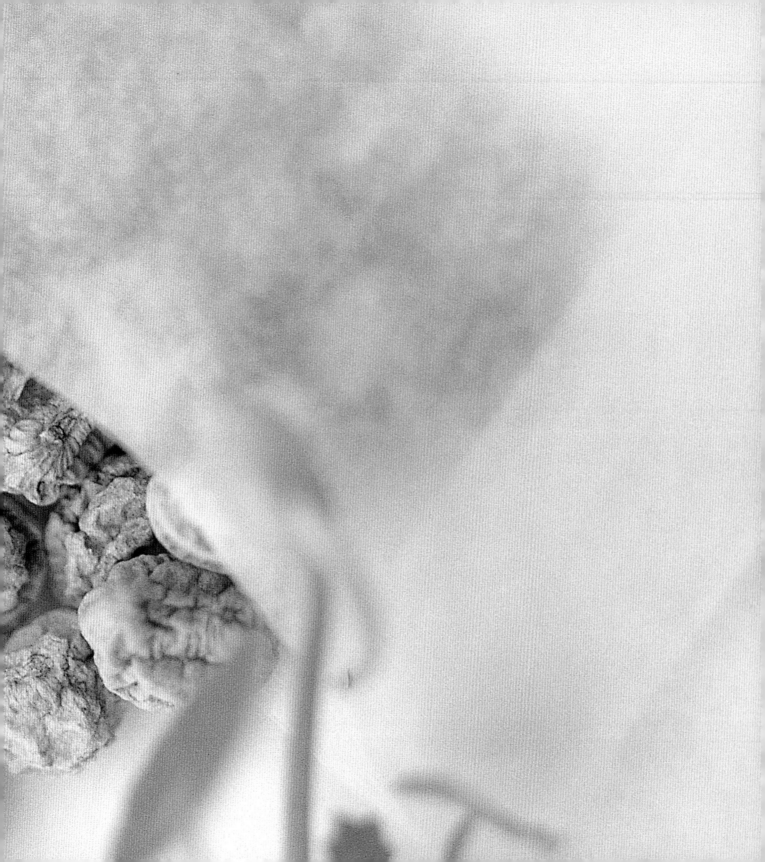

Graceful Vines

FRAGRANT SWEET PEA BOUQUETS IN RIOTS OF MIXED COLORS, MASSED IN SINGLE MUTED tones of palest cream or lavender, or gathered into small clutches of deep, dark reds or maroons, signal spring to me. Although the long-stemmed blossoms are more versatile than the short-stemmed ones, don't disregard the latter, as even the shortest stems can be clustered together to make a bouquet. Consider, too, not picking single stems at all, but lengths of flowering vines to use in large, wild arrangements.

In England, sweet peas are nearly a mania with gardeners and have been for over a century. One British seed company alone lists over two hundred varieties, and new introductions are eagerly awaited by aficionados. It is estimated that close to four thousand sweet peas have been given individual names. At the Chelsea Flower Show, held every May in London, an entire stand is given over to a sweet pea competition with a hundred or so blooms each of the competing varieties gathered into displayed bunches to be judged by rigorous standards: trueness of color and freshness of bloom, placement of bloom, size and form of bloom, stem proportionate to size of bloom, and effectiveness of staging.

Even though nasturtiums are not commonly thought of as bouquet flowers and are not part of a national passion, they share similarities with sweet peas. Both are vining and can be trained on trellises, strings, twigs, or fences, and both produce prolifically. Individual flower stems or blooming lengths of vine can be cut. An added attraction of nasturtiums is their beautiful round, lily-pad-like leaves on long stems. These too can be cut singly or left on the sinuously curling vine for bouquets.

Like sweet peas, nasturtiums have large seeds, are extremely easy to grow, and are suitable for containers as well as for garden planting. Both flowers prefer cool to moderate growing conditions, eschewing too much summer heat, and are long lasting in water once cut. But the similarity ends when it comes to colors. The nasturtiums are bright orange, gold, shocking crimson, and scarlet, with occasional cream and salmon tints. No lavender or pale pink here.

Sweet peas and nasturtiums are both annuals, but in temperate climates like that of Southern California, where I grew up, nasturtiums perform as perennials. Elsewhere, in all but the mildest climates, they are killed by the first frost. Sweet peas, in contrast, can survive light frost and are frequently planted in fall in areas with mild winter climates, although they are typically planted in early spring. These versatile, simple flowers will produce lavish bouquets throughout their season, even for first-time gardeners.

*Since sweet peas bloom in
spring and early summer, and
in some instances in fall, and
nasturtiums bloom nearly
year-round in some areas, but
certainly in summer and fall,
a vast number of shrubs and
other flowers are in season at
the same time. Look for lilacs,
flowering fruit trees, tulips,
branches of green fruits or
nuts, and late daffodils for
combining with spring sweet
peas. Summer nasturtiums
might be mixed with other
summer-flowering plants
and shrubs, such as zinnias,
berries on the vine, roses,
sunflowers, and geraniums.
In fall, branches of orange
persimmons and maple
leaves, rudbeckias, and
chrysanthemums are among
the possibilities.*

*In this spring bouquet,
'Mammoth' sweet peas are
accented with clusters of
green almonds and their
leaves.*

SWEET PEA

Outside England, gardeners see only the smallest bit of the huge number of sweet pea colors and flowering types, although seeds for some of them can be obtained through specialty flower catalogs such as Thompson & Morgan, an English seed company that produces an American edition of their catalog. Not only do the colors include nearly every shade of pink, rose, salmon, red, crimson, purple, cream, white, and even blue, but there are also specific bicolor, variegated types and one called a wire type. On the latter, a fine, fine line, like the wire of a delicate French ribbon, ripples along the outermost edge of the two lower wing petals and the standard or upper petal in the back, while the remaining petals—the two that form the keel, and the two that fold around it, the wing petals—are variegated.

Sweet peas are categorized as tall and dwarf or semidwarf, with two main tall types, the English Spencer and the American. The latter produces more blooms and has a greater tolerance for heat. Some of the old-fashioned varieties of both types, and newer ones bred from those lines, have an especially pronounced fragrance. Regardless of type, it is essential to keep sweet peas cut as blossoms appear to prolong the flowering season. If left on the vine, spent flowers quickly form seedpods, signaling to the plant that its life cycle is completing and it can begin to shut down. The result will be fewer and fewer flowers, an increasing number of flat green seedpods, and a declining plant. You may, however, choose at some point to let the sweet peas dry down and go to seed, then harvest and save the seeds to plant the following year, with some to give away.

In addition to color and size, sweet peas are grouped by their time of flowering—early or late—and by their resistance to heat. In general, they perform best in temperate to cool growing conditions, and tend to bloom less, lose their clarity of color, and be less fragrant when the weather is hot and dry.

The time of planting is determined primarily by individual growing conditions. In my Mediterranean climate, it is best to plant sweet peas in fall. The plants grow several inches and then

Sweet Pea Trellising

weet peas will attach to string, wire, a trellis, even to twigs, automati-

ally wrapping their tendrils and vines around whatever support is

rovided. As they continue to grow, the vines may reach six feet or

ore. Use a six-foot twiggy tree branch in the English manner, or wire

string netting supported on strong poles or attached to a fence.

engths of string, twine, or wire may be used against a fence or other

upport as well. In all cases, anchor the support well or the heavy

nes will topple it.

SEED SOAKING

Sweet pea seeds that are black or have a variegated seed coat are hard seeds, and germination can be speeded by soaking them overnight in water before planting. Nasturtiums too have hard-coated seeds, and they benefit from overnight soaking as well.

patiently wait over winter for warming spring days. Once the temperature rises, the plants grow quickly, and the first flowers appear in late March or early April. I have also planted in December, when the ground was not too wet, and those sweet peas bloom by early May. Early May often brings hot weather, however, and June always does, so in order to have a longer season of bloom, I prefer fall planting. Elsewhere, where cooler summer climates reign, summer sweet peas flourish.

Sweet pea seeds vary in size, but are generally considered large seeds, ranging from the size of pellets for a BB gun to silver candy sprinkles. The plants perform best in a location with rich, well-drained soil and full sun, although they can tolerate three-quarters of a day of full sun. Sow the seeds three-quarters to one inch deep and space them four to six inches apart, including the dwarf bush varieties. Standard sweet pea vines are generally provided supports for the vines to twist around as they grow. A trellis, strings, wires, nets, even twiggy tree prunings will perform this function. Sweet peas can also be left, if you have the space, to spread and grow out, flat and unpropped.

Sow the seeds in fall in mild winter climates for spring bloom, and in late winter and early spring for late spring and early summer bloom. Elsewhere, plant the seeds as soon as the ground can be worked.

Keep the ground moist until the seeds germinate. Thereafter, maintain water in the root zone. Fertilize with a dilute liquid fertilizer or manure tea once the seedlings have six to eight true leaves. Fertilize again every three weeks. Particularly annoying sweet pea pests are the birds that eat the young seedlings, and snails and slugs. Unfortunately, birds seem controllable only by netting, but I have found that by disguising my sweet pea plantings with a jungle of twigs and leaves, they can grow to a foot or more in secrecy. By the time they are that large, the birds leave them alone.

Although sweet peas may be started from transplants, they are so easily and so successfully grown from seed, I recommend seed-sowing them.

SAVING SWEET PEA SEEDS

When the pods are full and drying and the lowest pods on the vine are just starting to crack open, cut the stems. Put the whole plants in a place where the seeds from the shattering pods will not be scattered and lost. This is easy to do outside on a tarp in dry areas, but where that isn't possible, put the plants loosely into open paper bags. Once the uppermost pods are dry enough to break open, thresh out all the seeds by hand or even by walking on the plants. Remove the dry plant matter and broken seeds by hand or by screening or blowing until only whole seeds are left. Deformed, unfilled seeds will probably not germinate, but it may be too painstaking to remove all of them. Spread the cleaned seeds in a shallow layer to dry until they are hard and shatter when tapped with a hammer. Pack the seeds in relatively airtight cans or plastic bags and store them in a cool, dry place, well protected from rodents.

For container plantings, choose dwarf or tall varieties, deciding whether or not to provide support for the tall ones or to let them cascade. The container should be at least eighteen inches deep and eighteen inches across. The seeding and maintenance instructions are the same as those for garden-planted sweet peas.

For longest vase life, cut sweet peas stems when the uppermost blossom is still a bud. These will last up to four to five days in water, and for six to seven days in a floral preservative. To harvest sweet peas on the vine, choose those that have a least one stem with several open blossoms. Not all the buds on all the stems will open once cut, but some will. The vines may exhibit some end wilting of the young tip growth, but several hours in water will revive them. Vines will last five or six days in water, and several days longer in floral preservative.

Not only are there numerous varieties of annual sweet peas but there are also several different races or types to consider, plus the perennials, which are outside the subject of this book. The types are Spencer, American, and dwarf. The basis for the modern sweet pea with wavy petals is the Spencer, which was developed and introduced in England in the early nineteen hundreds, and was preceded by selections of flat-petaled types that were improvements of the original wild sweet pea that came to England from Sicily or perhaps Malta. The Spencers have flowers that are generally smaller and fewer to the stem—two or three in the older varieties, and four or five in the newer ones—than the American types. They have an extensive color range, significant fragrance, and limited tolerance for heat. The American types are multiflowering, producing long, strong stems with five to nine large blooms on each stem, and are easygoing when it comes to heat. Most bloom earlier than the Spencers, and include the winter-flowering sweet peas that are so successful in Southern California and similar climate areas in Australia and New Zealand. Dwarf sweet peas have a nonclimbing, bushy growing habit and are primarily American types with similar flowers and colors.

SPENCER

The varieties of Spencers listed here are some of my personal favorites, but there are many, many more from which to choose, in a huge selection of colors. Late Spencers with vines reaching a height of six to eight feet are a popular choice among cut-flower growers.

Old Spice (*Lathyrus odoratus*) is a mixture of old sweet types akin to those that preceded the Spencers. The small flowers carry a sweet and powerful fragrance, and bloom singly or in twos or threes in bicolored variations of intense to pale lavender and maroon, light pink and dark. The vines may reach eight feet high and the plants are quite heat resistant.

Royal Wedding (*L. odoratus*) has large, snow-bright, sweetly scented blooms on long stems.

Unwins Mixed Stripes (*L. odoratus*) is a spectacular mixture of a number of different bicolored flowers in shades of deep carmine, navy blue, maroon, lavender, and bright and pale pink. The background is generally white and the petals finely edged and splashed with stripes in a contrasting color. It is nearly honey scented and the stems are of medium length.

Sea Wolf (*L. odoratus*) bunched in a bouquet looks like an undulating wave of palest lavender. It usually bears four fragrant blooms on each of its relatively long stems.

Flagship (*L. odoratus*) is deep, dark, fragrant purple with medium to long stems.

Spencer Mixed (*L. odoratus*) contains an elegant selection of colors, mostly in shades of purple, pink, and lavender, with a scattering of red and, of course, white. They are quite fragrant and the stems are medium to long.

AMERICAN

Cuthbertson Mixed (*L. odoratus*) is a good, standard variety with a fine range of colors that includes lavender, pale pink, rose, scarlet, white, salmon, and purple. The blooms are large and fill the stems. It has a slight perfume and some resistance to heat.

Royal Family Mixed (*L. odoratus*) is an improved version of 'Cuthbertson,' flowering about two weeks earlier and generally with larger blooms on longer stems. It shows some resistance to heat and has a light fragrance. The mix contains lavender, white, pink, deep rose, and maroon. These colors are also available singly.

Royal Family Maroon (*L. odoratus*) is a deep, dark wine color, and one of my favorites.

Winter Elegance (*L. odoratus*) is an early bloomer, coming into flower two to three weeks before most other varieties. It is quite fragrant and has large, lush blooms on long stems. It is available in pink, lavender, white, or salmon.

DWARF BUSH

Knee-Hi Mix (*L. odoratus*) is bushy, growing to slightly over two feet in a classic color range that includes pastels and deep colors. The stems are of medium length, and the fragrance is delicate. It is slightly less heat tolerant than 'Supersnoop.'

Supersnoop (*L. odoratus*) a heat-tolerant variety, grows to a bushy two and one-half feet, but has no tendrils. It is quite floriferous and fragrant, and exhibits blooms in red, white, pink, and lavender with some purple.

NASTURTIUM

The nasturtium is thought of as a landscape plant, but the flowers make wonderful bouquets. Single stems, buds, long-stemmed leaves, and lengths of vines all can be cut and slipped into vases. The colors of most varieties are gold, orange, and red, but there are also pale cream, mahogany, and bicolors available. The flowers have spurs, the little curving tip at the base from which children suck the nectar. The leaves are generally bright green, but one variety has green-and-cream leaves, and another has deep, dark blue-green ones. Vining, semivining, and bush dwarf types, plus single and double flowers, add to the variation in these old-fashioned plants. One dwarf bush type, 'Whirlybird,' produces flowers that rise up above the leaves in a tidy clump, making it an excellent choice for container planting. The flowers of the vining types twist and curl within the vines and generally have curving stems rather than upright ones like those of 'Whirlybird.'

The plants will bloom profusely from early summer through to the first frost. They are not at all frost tolerant, and with the first drop of the temperature to freezing, the plants will flop. But they are easy to grow from seed, so you shouldn't mind replanting year after year. In areas where freezes do not occur, nasturtiums act as perennials, blooming nearly year-round.

Few pests or diseases besiege nasturtiums, but if the soil is too rich or if the plants are too heavily watered, they will grow vegetatively without blooming. Poor soil and little or no fertilizer suit nasturtiums. Keep the undergrowth of dried leaves cleared away, as this is a favorite habitat of mice.

WATER LEVELS

Since flowers continue to respire and grow after they are cut, they should be held in clean water that is kept refilled. Dirty water and bacteria will clog the vessels in the stem and reduce the capacity of the plant to lift water. Check the water levels of your containers at least once a day, more often if the containers are small, and maintain the original levels. If you are using floral foam in your container, make sure that it remains saturated.

The wrinkled seeds are the size of large peas, which makes them easy to handle and to space in the garden. Except in very hot growing conditions, where a half day of sun is preferred, nasturtiums are best planted in a location with three-quarters to a full day of sun. If there is not enough sun, the nasturtiums produce few, if any, flowers. Plant the seeds one-half inch deep, spacing them four to six inches apart for the bush types and eight to ten inches apart for the vining ones. They may be sown any time of the year in frost-free areas. In mild winter climates, plant from early spring throughout July. In areas with cold winter climates, sow the seeds when all danger of frost has passed. In areas with short growing seasons, start them inside in flats or small pots and transplant them in the outdoors when the chill is gone.

NASTURTIUM SALAD

The flowers, buds, and leaves of nasturtiums have a delightful peppery flavor, which is a welcome addition to salads. To make a salad, remove the stems from two cups of small leaves. Add a handful of buds and the petals of a dozen blossoms. Combine these with a cup of baby lettuce leaves and toss with a vinaigrette dressing and a sprinkle of freshly ground black pepper.

Both the dwarf and the vining types are best grown in containers at least twelve inches deep and twelve inches in diameter, although I have successfully cultivated them in window boxes only eight inches deep. The seeding instructions are the same as for garden-grown plants, but container-grown nasturtiums will require an application of dilute liquid fertilizer every ten days to two weeks during the leafy growth, and thereafter only if the leaves begin to yellow.

Cut nasturtiums when in bud form, once the bud has cracked and color is showing, or when partially or fully opened. The cut stems and vines will last three to four days in water, or five to six days with a floral preservative.

VINING

Climbing Nasturtium (*Tropaeolum majus*) has long, trailing vines reaching fifteen feet and longer. In coastal California it climbs and winds around the old wooden garages of the beach towns, across and over backyard fences, atop low roofs, and up into the fronds of palm trees. The flowers are shades of orange, yellow, gold, and red, with an occasional cream or mahogany.

Glorious Gleam (*T. majus*) is actually semivining and is similar to 'Climbing Nasturtium,' but its growth habit is slightly more tame and the vines typically grow to only eight feet. The colors are the same, however, and some of the flowers are double.

DWARF

Whirlybird (*T. minus*), a hybrid strain, has upright flowers and grows in a compact mound, and the flowers are spurless. It is available in single colors of 'Cherry Rose,' 'Gold,' 'Mahogany,' 'Orange,' 'Scarlet,' 'Tangerine,' and 'Cream,' and in a mixture of all seven colors.

Empress of India (*T. majus*) has unusual, deep blue-green leaves and dark red flowers, and although a dwarf, it produces short vines two to three feet long.

Alaska (*T. majus*) displays leaves variegated in cream and apple green. At first glance it appears that the leaves are not healthy, and although interesting looking, this is not a nasturtium to my taste. Like 'Empress of India,' it has short vines two to three feet long.

Peaches and Cream (*T. majus*) is a pale yellow cream blossom with a splash of orange at the throat. The plant itself has a mounding growth habit with some short vines.

Spitfire (*T. majus*) has bright scarlet flowers and equally bright green foliage. It is a particularly good choice for container planting because, while a bush type, it does produce short, cascading vines.

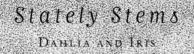

Stately Stems

Dahlia and Iris

Stately Stems

EVEN THOUGH IRISES AND DAHLIAS ARE VERY DIFFERENT IN BOTH THEIR GROWTH HABIT and flower shapes, they bring to bouquets their shared characteristic of stiff, elegant stems. Whether the stems are cut long or short, the flower heads remain well set on the top, like a hat on a woman with perfect posture.

Dahlias were the source of a flower craze in England and Europe during the mid-eighteen hundreds, so plant breeders, professional and amateur alike, set out to hybridize the single-petaled, red flower native of Mexico. Within a few short years there were double-petaled red flowers, which were soon followed by blooms in various sizes, petal forms, and colors. Today, hundreds more named varieties appear each year, offering the backyard gardener a near-overwhelming array of choices.

In the eighteenth and nineteenth centuries, ruffled bearded irises (also called German, flag, or pogon irises) were a source of fascination for French and English plant breeders as they set about to create new colors and to increase the size of these voluptuous flowers. The French seed house of Vilmorin was particularly active, breeding dozens of new varieties in multiple colors, and then having artists paint them for the folio catalog the company displayed in their seed-and-plant shop in Paris.

Dutch iris, a latecomer with a smooth, narrow flower head, has a more limited color range than the bearded iris and is most often found in shades of purple, blue, yellow, and brown. This iris is far more commonly available in the floral trade than the bearded, which is considered a specialty flower.

REFRESHING DROOPING
BOUQUETS

When a room is quite warm, flowers tend to droop if they lose their moisture. A bouquet can often be refreshed by removing it overnight to a cool place, such as a garage, cellar, or basement, or by periodically spraying it with a misting bottle.

Both dahlias and irises are grown from bulbs. Technically, dahlias grow from tuberous roots, bearded irises from rhizomes, and Dutch irises from true bulbs. For the gardener, this is good news, because bulbs store within themselves the energy to grow and bloom for one season, requiring only warmth and water from the garden. For good growth the following year, they will require a moderate amount of fertilizer. Dahlias are planted in spring and flower from summer until the frosts of fall. Bearded irises are planted in late summer or early fall and bloom in late spring and early summer, although some varieties, called remontant or rebloomers, may bloom again in fall. Dutch irises are planted in fall for spring and early summer bloom, but commercial growers force them to bloom out of season so that flower markets enjoy a near-year-round supply.

In spring and early summer,
poppies, lupines, tulips, daffodils,
snowdrops, roses, lilacs, magnolias, flowering fruit trees,
wisteria, foxgloves, delphiniums,
larkspurs, blue lace flowers,
Queen Anne's lace, nasturtiums,
violets, and dogwood are among
the multitude of flowers and
shrubs in bloom. Come high
summer, sunflowers, cleomes,
bachelor's buttons, hollyhocks,
fruits on branches, daisies, and
geraniums are part of the season's
panoply. Fall brings the changing
foliage of maple, pistachio,
persimmon, and walnut trees
to mix into bouquets.

Branches of still-green
persimmons mix with Rosa rugosa
rose hips, leaves and fruits of
black mission figs, and 'Amber
Queen' and 'Brookside Cheri'
dahlias to create a late
summer bouquet.

DAHLIA

I fell in love with dahlias upon seeing a photograph of a magnificent walled garden full to overflowing with an artist's dahlia collection. The photograph was taken in misty morning light and the blossoms were a veritable sea of shimmering color. For a time I became obsessed with dahlias, pouring through thick catalogs and making extensive lists, imagining my dahlia garden.

It was not a success. The flowers grew well enough, but I had planted them too far apart on too rigid a grid pattern, and the result entirely lacked the wild, mystical look of the garden that had inspired me. I tried again, this time planting the tubers close together, in a more random fashion, and letting nigellas grow underfoot. It was a far more satisfactory arrangement, and now I thoroughly enjoy loading my basket with long stems bearing buds and opening blooms. Each year I add a few new varieties to my collection.

Dahlias are among the most varied of flowers for bouquets because of their range of size, form, and color. Literally every imaginable color and shade, except blue and green, are available. Pinks, salmons, dark reds, purples, bright oranges, multicolored, bicolored—all are represented in a rarely repeating pattern. Over the years, the sizes and forms have been classified, and while the classifications might seem arcane, they are useful in helping to choose the style of dahlia to grow. The American Dahlia Society recognizes twelve official classifications of dahlias. The widest range of varieties is available in the three cactus classifications—the incurved cactus, semicactus, and straight cactus—plus the formal and informal decorative. Pompon, single, collarette, anemone, ball, peony, and miscellaneous make up the remaining classifications. My favorites are the cactus, decorative, and pompon.

Cactus dahlias, which have layers and layers of petals, are one of the most popular types. The petals of the incurved cactus are rolled the full length, and the tips of the petals turn back toward the center of the flower. Semicactus blooms have petals that are flat at the base, curling less than half their length, while the petals of straight cactus are rolled only half their length. The sizes of cactus dahlias range from two inches across to over a foot, but the small and midsized flowers are easier to handle in bouquets than the huge, dinner-plate sizes are.

The heavily petaled decorative class of dahlias demonstrates the same range of size as the cactus, but within two rather than three categories, formal and informal. The informals are my preference here, displaying a certainly irregularity in petal length, shape, and formation. Some are short, some are long, some curled, some flat. The formal dahlias have flat, evenly spaced petals.

Pompon dahlias are small—two inches in diameter or less—and their tightly furled or quilled petals are layered to form a near perfectly rounded flower head. These small flowers fit easily into bouquets, where they may play either a central or supporting role.

The size of dahlia plants varies as much as the petal shape, ranging from two and a half feet to five feet. Those that are less than two feet tall are dwarf dahlias. All dahlias, though, regardless of size or shape, require a location with full sun and a loose soil, preferably manured or composted. The biggest threat to successful dahlia growing is root rot, caused by poor soil drainage.

Dahlias can be grown from seed, planted in early spring, but tubers, which resemble small, dark brown sweet potatoes and are often sold in a cluster of three or four, are easier to grow and offer a much greater choice of colors and shapes. The planting location should receive a full day of sun, as these heat-loving flowers do not flourish in semishade. If the tubers are in clumps, separate them and then put them into the ground sideways, each six inches deep and eighteen inches apart. Dahlias are highly frost sensitive, so do not plant the tubers until after the last frost. If the ground is dry when

DIGGING AND STORING DAHLIA TUBERS

If you live in an area that has hard frosts, it will be necessary to dig up the dahlia tubers and store them over the winter. When the plant tops have turned brown, or about two weeks after a hard frost, cut the stalks back to four to six inches. Using a garden fork, gently lift the tubers from the soil. Shake or wash the dirt from them, then leave them in the air for a few hours until the skin is dry. Pack them into boxes heavily lined with newspaper, then top them with sand, peat moss, or sawdust. Do not use plastic to cover them because they will rot. Store the packed box in a cool, dry place until spring, and time to plant again.

LOCK-TOP BAGS

To protect a special container, or one that is not watertight, heavy-duty plastic lock-top bags can be partially filled with water and placed inside of it. Put the flowers into the bag, and zip up the sides as needed to hold the flowers in place. Floral clay can be used to attach the bag to the sides of the container, to hold it upright and prevent spillage.

you plant, water thoroughly once and, if spring rains are sparse, water again when the first shoots emerge. When the plants are growing, maintain water in the root zone, preferably by watering at the base rather than with overhead sprinklers, which can break the stems and branches of mature plants. Fertilizing should be done at the time of planting, with a low-nitrogen fertilizer such as 5–10–10 or 10–20–20. Too much nitrogen will impede bloom quantity and size.

In areas with mild winter climates, like mine, leave dahlias in the ground to overwinter, to bloom again the following summer. Elsewhere, they will need to be dug up and stored, then replanted again in late spring. Dahlias have stiff, brittle stems, so the larger plants may require support to protect them from breaking in strong winds or rainstorms.

Most dahlias may be grown in large containers at least twenty-four inches deep and twenty-four inches in diameter.

For longest vase life, blossoms should be cut when they are three-quarters to nearly fully open. Dip the cut stems in two to three inches of very hot water, then allow them to cool for several hours in the water. The cut flowers will last three to four days in water, and up to five to six days with a floral preservative.

Many, many kinds of dahlias are available, so I have chosen to list some that I find particularly beautiful and easy to grow for bouquets, rather than attempting to include selections from all of the thirteen classifications one readily finds in bulb catalogs. Dahlias have been so extensively hybridized that they are recognized horticulturally by genus and shared characteristics rather than by the more typical scientific classification of genus and species.

CACTUS

Brookside Cheri, a straight cactus, has lush salmon pink blooms with faintly gold tones at the petal base. The flowers are six inches across, growing on branching plants that reach four feet.

Romance, a straight cactus, has peach-colored petals with creamy white centers. The flowers are three inches across, growing on branching plants that reach four feet.

DECORATIVE

White Swan is a formal decorative with bright white, tightly packed petals. The flowers are four inches across and bloom on branching plants that reach to three and one-half feet.

Midnight Dancer is a formal decorative of deep purple-fuchsia. The flowers reach seven inches across on a rather compact plant that grows to three and one-half feet.

POMPON

Amber Queen is a pompon of golden orange, with two-inch round flowers growing on branching plants that reach four feet. Support is helpful.

Koko Puff is a pompon in an unusual color of pale lavender with tones of tan. The flower is small, only one and one-half inches across, growing on a compact, three-foot plant.

BEARDED IRIS

Both bearded and Dutch irises are superb bouquet flowers, and the ease with which they can be grown makes them a good choice for the backyard gardener. They both have attractive, sword-shaped leaves, with those of the bearded iris quite wide, and those of the Dutch narrow and strapping. These leaves can be added to bouquets along with the flowers.

I first acquired bearded irises one fall when I stopped in front of a house whose fifty-foot-long, four-foot-wide walkway of tall, pale lavender irises I had always admired. A little sign stuck in the bed next to paper sacks read, "Iris. $2 a bag." I bought all eight bags, each with ten rhizomes, brought them home, and set to digging a place for them.

The iris flower itself, regardless of variety, is composed of six segments arranged in two sets of three. In the upper segment are petals, and these are called standards. The lower segment is composed of sepals, called falls. In the case of the bearded iris, the falls have a narrow furry strip running down the center, hence the term *bearded*.

Although there are a number of sizes of bearded irises, the most dramatic ones in bouquets are the standard and tall types that grow to between two and one-half and four feet. (Bearded irises are classified by height as border bearded, intermediate bearded, miniature divary bearded, miniature tall bearded, standard tall bearded, and tall bearded.) The stems bear as many as five or six buds, which unfurl one after the other. Although most bearded irises bloom in spring and early summer, some, called remontant or rebloomers, also flower in late summer and fall. Often the reblooming aspect is linked to climate and growing region rather than to a specific variety.

Bearded irises require a location with a half to three-quarters a day of full sun. Filtered light, especially in areas with hot summers, is welcomed by the plants, and some colors, such as the browns

Dividing the Rhizomes of Bearded Irises

Bearded irises continually produce new rhizomes, and these can be dug and divided every few years, thus increasing the planting. The best time to do this is in midsummer, when the new roots and budding rhizomes have started to develop and are clearly evident and easily distinguished from the older rhizomes, which are darker. Dig the rhizomes and wash them. Select those that have new bud growth for replanting, separating them from the old rhizomes with a sharp knife. Dust the cuts with sulfur before replanting to discourage infection. Cut the leaf fans to within four inches of the rhizome. Plant as described in the text, and keep the ground moist until new growth emerges.

and pale yellows, are more brilliant and fade less than if planted in full, direct sun. I have two beds of bearded irises, both planted beneath trees that are just barely leafing out when the irises are blooming in April and May, giving them some protection from what can be a very hot sun.

The rhizomes should be planted shallowly, with no more than an inch of soil covering them. In old beds, the rhizomes were often left exposed because it was believed that was the best way to plant them. Today, though, dig down to a depth of about five inches, then make little ridges of soil, each about ten inches apart. Place the rhizomes on the ridges and spread out their roots. Since growth starts from the ends with leaves, point those ends in the desired direction of growth. Pack the earth tightly around the roots and the tubers, leaving no air pockets, and then water. If the weather is dry, water periodically until new growth appears and keep well watered during bloom. In spring, before the plants show new growth, feed them with a balanced fertilizer. In midsummer, cut back the leaves to within four inches of the soil and fertilize again, lightly.

Bearded irises may be successfully grown in large containers at least twenty-four inches deep and twenty-four inches in diameter.

Irises may be cut when the first buds are starting to unfurl, or later when one or more buds are already open. Once cut and brought indoors the flowers will continue to open. Plunging their stems into cold water and leaving them in a cool place for several hours before placing them in the house will prolong their vase life, which is up to four days. If floral preservative is added, they may last five to six days.

As with dahlias, there are so many, many varieties from which to choose that I am only offering a selection here of some of the different color combinations available. Bearded irises are divided into five classifications of color patterns. These are self, which means both the standards and the falls are the same color; plicata, or speckled flowers; freckled, flowers streaked or netted with a second color; bicolor, where the standards are one color, the falls another; bitone, where the standards and falls are two values of the same color; and finally, blends that display two or more colors mixed. The beards themselves may be yellow, orange, blue, or salmon. For serious fanciers of bearded irises, the beard color is as intriguing as the colors of the flowers themselves.

The extensively hybridized bearded irises are recognized horticulturally by genus and shared characteristics rather than the more typical scientific classification of genus and species. The following varieties are all tall bearded irises.

Gay Parasol has pale blue standards and deep purple falls.

Masada is primarily maroon blending to shocking pink at the base. The standards are bronze, as are the edges of the falls. The beard is a delicate bronze.

Tequila Sunrise has sunset orange standards, a fall of soft lavender edged in tan, and a beard of gold. It grows to about three feet.

Dover Beach has white standards with light blue falls and grows to three feet.

Edith Wolford has yellow standards and blue falls and grows to nearly four feet.

Butterscotch Brown is a soft, warm golden brown growing to three feet.

DUTCH IRIS

Relatively new to the flower world, Dutch irises were hybridized by Dutch breeders in the early twentieth century by crossing the Spanish iris with numerous other iris species to produce an orchidlike flower, commonly grown today for the floral trade and in home gardens. The stiff, upright stems can be cut short for small, dinner-table bouquets, or left their full length, usually twelve to sixteen inches, to use in larger settings.

The earlier hybrids were primarily purple, but today we find them in various color combinations, with falls of light blue and standards of purple, creamy falls with pure white standards, and self colors of soft brown and lavender, usually with yellow or orange blotches on the throats of the falls.

A location with full sun and well-drained soil is ideal for Dutch irises, although some filtered shade is acceptable in areas that may be hot in late spring and early summer when the flowers appear. Plant them in the fall between September and November. Dig holes twice the depth of a bulb, about four inches, and place the bulbs with their pointed tips facing upward. Position them one inch apart, and cover with soil. Water immediately after planting if the ground is dry, and during growth and bloom in spring and summer. Fertilize at the time of planting, and again once all the flowers are cut. The flowers will return to bloom again the next year or treat them as annuals, buying new bulbs each year.

Dutch irises grow well in containers that may be of any diameter, but at least eight inches deep. Follow the same planting and maintenance instructions used for garden planting.

Dutch irises, the result of much hybridization, are recognized by genus and shared characteristics rather than the more typical scientific classification of genus and species.

Cream Beauty has white standards and creamy yellow falls with a bright orange blotch.

Sapphire Beauty has deep purple standards, paler purple falls, and a golden blotch.

Oriental Beauty has lavender-blue standards, golden amber falls, and a barely discernible yellow blotch.

Rusty Beauty has honey brown standards with lighter falls and no visible blotch.

CUTTING DUTCH IRISES

A new batch of Dutch irises, called the 'Beauty series,' offers an extensive range of colors. All the flowers grow to a height of about twenty inches and are May and June bloomers.

Cut Dutch irises when the buds show a pencil width of color. Once cut, put the stems in warm (100 degrees F) water for several hours. Floral preservative does not extend the vase life of two to five days.

Artful Forms

Tulip, Daffodil, and Ranunculus

Artful Forms

TULIPS, DAFFODILS, AND RANUNCULUSES ARE AMONG THE MOST GRACEFUL AND ELEGANT of flowers, yet they retain a certain wild charm. Tulips begin to bloom on upright, inflexible stems, but once cut and brought inside, they reveal their sensuous appeal as the stems elongate, curve, and bend toward the light. The flowers continue to open for several days, and even their fallen petals are attractive as they lay at the base of the vase, having left behind the long stamens and the seed heads, artful forms themselves.

The shape of a daffodil, like that of a calla lily, fascinated the artists of both the art nouveau and art deco periods, so fanciful, stylized versions of the flowers are found in paintings, ironwork, and stained glass of those eras. When in bud, the heads of daffodils and tulips bend downward, gradually lifting as they open and bloom, lending a certain movement to bouquets.

The heavily petaled and ruffled flowers of the big, showy blossoms of the Tecolote ranunculus are one of the most spectacular of cut flowers, but unlike daffodils and tulips, these are a relatively recent development, having been bred only in the last forty years. Their plump, buttonlike buds stand upright on long and often curving stems, and the flowers remain upright as they open, but the weight of the larger flowers will gracefully bend their stems.

Tulips, daffodils, and ranunculuses are all bulbs. They are put into the ground in fall or early winter in most climates; in areas with harsh winters, ranunculuses are planted in spring. Their period of bloom, depending upon the variety, ranges from February, even January for some daffodils, on into May. The blooming season for tulips also varies with variety, with some as early as March and others as late as June. Ranunculuses are more predictable, and the Tecolote bloom continuously from April well into May and early June.

TULIP

Tulips are enormously rich in color, form, and size. The entire color spectrum is represented, save blue. Red, rose, pink, lavender, white, purple, and every shade in between, plus bicolor, striped, and variegated all appear. Some varieties are single, some double, peony petaled, lily-shaped, or scalloped, in addition to the classic tulip shape. Sizes range from the tiny species tulips, many only six inches tall, to late single tulips with two-foot stems.

Species tulips, sometimes listed in bulb catalogs as botanical tulips, are the wild tulips from which the modern hybrids were bred, and their origins lie in places such as Turkistan, Baluchistan, Turkey, and Crete. Their diminutive size makes them perfect for small bouquets, although they are rarely found except in home gardens. Unlike the larger tulips, they are not part of the mainstream floral trade. Their leaves, petal shape, and coloration are varied. Some leaves, such as those of *Tulipa urumiensis,* are narrow, drooping, and thin, while those of *T. praestans* 'Unicum' are wide, wavy, and edged with white. They can be found with dark red stripes on wide, gray-green leaves, or leaves that are narrow and crinkly, silvery blue or gray-green, or smooth and silky green. Unlike most tulips, the species tulips will naturalize in moderate climates.

There are two official classifications of single tulips, early and late. The two resemble each other in flower form, but differ in height and time of bloom. The early singles are between twelve and eighteen inches and bloom in March and April, while the late singles are the tallest of all tulips, growing to twenty-six inches and blooming in May and into early June.

REVIVING WILTING TULIPS

Tulips whose stems have lost their strength, and whose heads are sagging, can be revived by immersing them overnight from flower head to stem tip in tepid water. A bathtub or a deep laundry sink is the ideal place to do this. The next morning they will have recovered their turgidity and look fresh and strong. Roses also respond to this simple technique.

In late winter, when the first daffodils bloom, witch hazel, flowering quince, hellebores, and violets are in season for gathering together in bouquets. With spring come lilacs, sweet peas, poppies, magnolias, fruit blossoms, blue lace flowers, love-in-a-mist, anemones, forget-me-nots, and nasturtiums, followed in early summer by peonies and the first roses.

Spring's pear blossoms mix with California poppies and white tulips to make this cup-size bouquet.

Other tulips that have single petals are the Triumph and Darwin, both of which bloom midseason, in late April and early May. The Darwin is the taller of the two, and because of its exceptionally sturdy stems, it has long been a popular florists' choice.

Among the other tulips are the early doubles, which are short stemmed, growing to about one foot, but with lush flowers blooming in late March and early April. The multipetaled peony tulips, which do indeed resemble their namesake, are May bloomers.

The lily-shaped tulips, with outward flaring petals, and the fringed varieties, with a shaggy edge around each petal, show off their stunning blossoms in May as well.

Parrot tulips, to my thinking, are the most striking members of the clan. They have huge petals, and when fully opened, create a flower nearly the size of a dinner plate. The petals themselves are crinkled, furled, and ruffled in the bud, and they open slowly, until finally the petals are flung back, spent and slightly smoothed. Their coloration is as notable as their shape, with variegations in two and sometimes three tones. These bloom in late April and May.

The bulbs of the species tulips are quite small, some no larger than the tip of a little finger, and often have tight-fitting skin. In contrast, the standard tulip bulbs are quite large and have a loose, papery skin.

The planting location should be sunny, although some shade may be tolerated in those areas that are liable to have a hot spring and early summer. A rule of thumb is to plant the bulbs at a depth of at least twice their diameter. So, a two-inch bulb would be planted four inches deep, and a tiny species tulip bulb only an inch or two deep. I plant tulips right next to one another with no more than an inch or two between them, as I like a tightly massed planting rather than a scattered one. I treat the bulbs as annuals, buying new ones each year, because in my area only the species tulips

DOUBLE-LAYERED TULIPS IN CONTAINERS

Planting fifty tulip bulbs in two layers in a single container produces a magnificent, dense display of blossoms that can act as a small cutting garden, while still looking showy on a front porch or a balcony. I recommend a container eighteen inches in diameter and at least eighteen inches deep, with a drainage hole or holes. Place a layer of gravel in the bottom over the hole, then fill to within eight inches of the rim with wet potting mix. Place the bulbs, touching and pointed tip up, in a layer, completely covering the surface of the mix. Make a second layer by off-setting bulbs on top of the first layer. Cover with moist potting mix, making sure it is down between the bulbs, and fill the container to within one inch of the rim. Water to settle the potting mix. It should be thoroughly saturated. Place in a sunny location and keep well watered. Use bulbs of a single color or of two colors that bloom at the same time, as even different colors of the same types, parrot tulips for example, may produce blooms over a period of three weeks, leaving some spent when others are just coming up.

naturalize and reproduce. If you live in an area that has cold winters and you would like the tulips to naturalize, space them two or three inches apart. Some of the modern hybrids do not naturalize as well as the older varieties, such as the single early tulips. Water at the time of planting, and again thereafter to keep the ground moist but not soggy. In the usual course of things, winter and spring rains will provide adequate water.

In cold winter climates, plant tulips in fall, when the weather has turned, about two weeks before the first frosts. In areas with mild winters, plant in November. Bulb planters, either short or long handled, may be used to make the holes. Bulb augers are also available, or the holes may be dug with a trowel. Yet another method, which I use, is to dig the planting space to the required depth, then scatter the bulbs in it. This gives a random, wild look to the planting. Each bulb is turned upright, and then the planted area is covered with soil.

Few pests other than gophers and birds bother tulips. Birds will attack an exposed bulb and the very new shoots, while the gophers eat the bulb from underneath.

Cut a tulip when the bud shows full color, except Darwin tulips, which can be cut when only half colored. Place the flowers in water where the buds will continue to open for three or four days, and then stay open for another week before the petals fall, even without the addition of a floral preservative.

All tulips may be successfully grown in containers, provided they are given adequate water from the time of planting through bloom and are never allowed to dry out.

Of all of the tulips available, I am including here only a handful, all of them personal favorites that I grow every year. The nomenclature among tulips varies. The less-hybridized species of botanical tulips are recognized by genus and species, but the extensively hybridized tulips are recognized horticulturally by shared characteristics. Remember that for massed flowering in the garden, you should choose varieties that will bloom at the same time, and for continued cutting over a longer span, plant varieties that bloom sequentially from early spring to late summer. For bouquet making, both schemes are useful, as the first allows for the luxury of huge bouquets, while the latter ensures tulips on a near daily basis until their season is ended.

CHILLING TULIP BULBS

Tulip bulbs require chilling in order to initiate flowering, so many are shipped prechilled. Most bulb catalogs state whether or not their bulbs are prechilled, and nursery personnel should be able to advise as well. If in doubt, prechill the bulbs for six weeks before planting by putting them in paper bags and keeping them in the vegetable bin of a refrigerator. In areas with cold winter climates, nature does the chilling, but in areas with mild winters, prechilling is necessary.

SPECIES OR BOTANICAL TULIPS

Bright Gem (*Tulipa batalinii*) is a delicate sunset shade of orangish yellow, and the tiny classically formed buds grow on short five-inch stems. The leaves are gray-green, stiff, and rather waxy looking.

Other *T. batalinii* include 'Bronze Charm,' a rusty bronze, and the bright 'Red Jewel,' which, at eight inches, is one of the taller species tulips.

Unicum (*T. praestans*) is a multiflowered species that has many small, bright red flowers with throats of brilliant yellow growing on eight-inch stems. The wide leaves are almost as interesting as the flowers, variegated and edged with white.

T. turkestanica is another multiflowered species tulip with the unusual attribute of flowers that close at night, showing only the soft violet color of the outside of the petals. When open, the flowers exhibit a pale cream interior, framed by wide, grayish blue leaves. One of the smaller species tulips, it grows to only five inches.

Fireflame Tulip (*T. acuminata*), at twenty inches, is one of the tallest of the species tulips and one of the most interesting, looking like an exotic spider. Its long, thin petals of red and yellow and its thin, scant leaves twist and have crinkled edges.

Montana (*T. wilsonia*) exhibits deep crimson buds sheltered by beautiful crinkle-edged leaves that are gray-blue, striated with maroon. Although short, only six inches, this species tulip seems much taller because of its elegant shape.

STANDARD TULIPS

Generaal de Wet, a single early tulip that grows to sixteen inches, has sweetly scented deep orange blossoms that, as they unfold to full size, become a lovely peach.

Cassini is a midseason Triumph tulip that has pure, deep red blooms on eighteen-inch stems.

Kees Nellis, another midseason Triumph, sprouts classic bright yellow edging around red petals. Its height is eighteen inches.

Pink Impression is a midseason Darwin tulip in a shade of deepest pink. It reaches a height of twenty-two inches and blooms in midseason.

Silver Stream is a midseason Darwin tulip in cream, but tinged with shades of red, giving the blooms an almost frosted look. The leaves of this twenty-four-inch-tall tulip are variegated white and green.

Blue Aimable is a late-season, May-flowering tulip of deep, dark purple that grows up to twenty-four inches.

Flaming Parrot is my favorite of all the magnificent parrot tulips for its vibrant color and enormous blooms—eight inches across when fully opened—and stems twenty inches long. It is yellow, streaked with deep crimson, and like the other parrot tulips, the petals are slightly convoluted and fringed. It is a late-season bloomer.

Apricot Parrot exhibits peachy orange blossoms, with the outside of the petals streaked with green. It is a late-season bloomer.

Estella Rijnveld is white streaked with red, and 'Rijnveld' is a late-season bloomer.

DAFFODIL

*D*affodil and *narcissus* are terms sometimes used interchangeably for the same flowers. Narcissus is the common name for the spring- and winter-flowering bulb that bears dangling clusters of short-cupped white flowers, with some varieties being yellow or yellow in white. These include those types referred to as paper whites. Daffodil is the common name for the familiar trumpeted, or large-cupped flowers, with an extensive number of variations both in form and in color, from pure white to shades of pink, yellow, amber, orange, and cream with single, double, and short-cupped heads. The confusion comes from the fact that *narcissus* is also the Latin name for all the daffodils.

Leaving terminology aside, daffodils and narcissus are among the most rewarding of all flowers to grow and to cut. I think no other flower arranges as well as these do, in the sense that they arrange themselves. A handful of stems put into a jar or vase falls into a graceful fan shape. Nothing else is needed. Because they are bulbs, they have all the nutrients they need for one season of growth. They also readily naturalize in the garden, where they will produce profuse blooms yearly, with only a little assistance from you.

The bulbs themselves have a dark brown, papery covering and may be quite nearly as large as a lemon or, in the case of the species or wild daffodils, as small as a pistachio nut. Narcissus and daffodils are planted in early fall in most areas, but somewhat later in areas with mild winter climates.

The planting areas should have full sun. Choose large bulbs with double noses for the largest flowers. (These are labeled DNI.) Plant standard bulbs five or six inches deep and the smaller species bulbs only three to four inches deep, depending upon their size, with the pointed side or nose facing up. Bulb planters or a trowel may be used for digging the holes, but the mixture I prefer is the same one I use for tulip bulbs: I dig the planting space to the required depth, scatter the bulbs in it, turn them upright, and cover the planted area with soil. The result is a pleasantly untamed plot.

BOUQUET CONTAINERS

Almost anything can be used to hold a bouquet of flowers. Tea or demitasse cups, empty spice tins, small glasses, even milk cartons can hold clusters of small flowers with their stems cut short, such as zinnias, nasturtiums, even tulips and narcissus. Old milk bottles, mason jars, flour or sugar canisters, teapots, and pitchers make casual holders for handfuls of graceful poppies, daffodils, tulips, and sweet peas. Wooden crates, boxes, and baskets holding waterproof liners such as jars or glasses create striking containers for bouquets of bearded irises, masses of dahlias, or a clutch of ranunculuses.

One of my favorite vases is a tall, weathered urn-shaped basket with a handle that has a large glass jar set inside. In spring it holds long stems of tulips, and in summer and fall it is full of sunflowers, dahlias, cosmos, zinnias, and coreopsis, either singly or mixed with roses or whatever else is at hand. In winter I keep it filled with rosehips and narcissus.

Narcissus and daffodils naturalize readily. To leave space for this, plant the standard sizes six inches apart, and the smaller ones three inches apart. Or, if maximizing space and display is the goal, plant them nearly touching. Once the bulbs are covered with soil, water the planted area. The seasonal rains should supply all the further water needed for the plants to grow and bloom. Snails and slugs can be pests on the long succulent leaves of the plants.

Once the flowers have bloomed, allow the leaves to wither and die. As they do this, they are storing food in the bulbs for next year's growth. In late summer, fertilize with a balanced granular fertilizer to ensure nutrients for the following season's bloom.

Cut the single blossoms when color is showing but the bud is still closed. The necks will be bent down. For double-blossom varieties, wait to cut until the flowers have started to open. The cut blossoms will last four to six days, gradually opening in water. Floral preservative has little impact on the life of the flowers once cut. Since daffodils release a mucus after

cutting that is harmful to other flowers, including tulips, they should be kept alone in water for at least twelve and for up to twenty-four hours, with one or two changes of water. Once the flowers are removed, wash the stems clean of any clinging mucus. If you can't wait that long, let them stand in a solution of five drops of bleach to one quart of water for one hour before mixing them in arrangements with other flowers.

Daffodils and narcissus may be successfully grown in containers at least twelve inches deep and eight inches in diameter. For fullest show, they are best planted in double layers as described for tulips (see page 121). Let the leaves die back after bloom as described for garden-planted bulbs.

Many, many varieties of narcissus and daffodils exist, and new ones appear each year. The different types are grouped into eleven divisions or classes: trumpet, long-cupped, small-cupped, double, triandrus hybrids, cyclamineus hybrids, jonquilla hybrids, tazetta and tazetta hybrids, poeticus narcissus, species and species hybrids, and a miscellaneous group that includes a number of modern flower forms such as the split cup. All are splendid in bouquets.

Here are listed some daffodils and narcissus that I keep planted in my own garden. They represent a wide range of shapes and colors for bouquets, but not all the divisions are included.

Narcissus and daffodils are horticulturally recognized by genus and division rather than by the more typical genus and species.

TRUMPET

Trumpet daffodils have one flower per stem, and the trumpet, or cup, is longer or at least as long as the petals.

Mount Hood is pure white, grows to about fourteen inches, and is a faithful performer.

King Alfred is the old faithful of the garden, and has been a favorite choice since the era of Queen Victoria. It is bright, true yellow and grows to about sixteen inches.

LONG-CUPPED

Long-cupped daffodils resemble the trumpet daffodils and have one flower per stem. The cup is shorter than the length of the petal, but is at least one-third its length. This division has the greatest number of varieties.

Ambergate displays yellow-orange petals, a dark red cup, and grows to a stalwart eighteen inches tall.

Manon Lescaut is one I chose for its name, but I have not been disappointed by its appearance, which is striking. The petals are white, and the ruffled-edged cup is a lush apricot with pink undertones. The flowers grow atop eighteen-inch stems.

Salome also has a pink cup, but it is more coral than apricot, and it too is tall at eighteen inches.

The larger the tulip bulb, the larger the bloom and the more vigorous the plant. In the bulb trade, the sizes are regulated and are termed top size, first size, and second size. Top-size bulbs are twelve centimeters or more in circumference; the first size is eleven to twelve centimeters; and the second size is ten to eleven centimeters. Holland, the largest exporter of tulip bulbs, ships only these three sizes to the United States. Species tulips, which have very small bulbs, do not fall into these sizing categories.

Daffodil bulbs are sized DNI, DNII, and DNIII. DNI, the largest size, is sixteen centimeters plus in circumference; DNII is fourteen to sixteen centimeters; and DNIII is twelve to fourteen centimeters. The largest daffodil bulbs have two large "noses," or tips, from which the flower stems are produced, the mid-sized two smaller noses, and the small size only one nose.

Ranunculus bulbs are sized according to their diameter. Jumbo, the largest size, is seven centimeters plus; number 1 is six to seven centimeters; number 2 is five to six centimeters; and number 3 is four to five centimeters.

SMALL-CUPPED

Small-cupped daffodils, with one flower per stem, have short, small cups—no longer than one-third the petal length—and are sometimes so small they are referred to as buttons or eyes.

Barrett Browing has a brilliant orange cup, not too small, and creamy white petals. It grows to sixteen inches.

DOUBLE

Double daffodils have three forms: the cup is absent and replaced by more petals; the cup is completely filled rather than open; or the stamens take on leaflike shapes.

Cheerfulness is outstanding in this class. Clusters of flowers the color of thick, rich cream bloom upon fourteen-inch stems. They have a delicate fragrance.

TRIANDRUS

Triandrus daffodils are generally characterized by clusters of small flowers. Sometimes the petals are reflexed, bending back away from the center of the flower.

Thalia was the first narcissus I planted, entranced after having read about the fragrance of its delicate white flowers. It grows to sixteen inches.

TAZETTA

Tazetta daffodils, also referred to as the narcissus group, are notable for the heady fragrance of the clusters of flowers that bloom on each stem. The paper whites, those used for indoor forcing as well as outdoor bloom, belong to this group.

Geranium has clusters of cream petals with dark orange cups, and a deep, sweet fragrance. It grows to fourteen inches.

Grand Soleil d'Or is an old Victorian favorite with petals of bright yellow surrounding orange cups. I planted these along with 'Thalia' in my first plantings.

Chinese Sacred Lily has a deep, sweet fragrance that can scent an entire room. Not a lily at all, nor Chinese, this narcissus has petals of cream and cups of golden orange. The strappy leaves are floppy, unlike those of most other narcissus and daffodils, which are generally quite upright during the plants' period of bloom.

Galilee is an early blooming paper white that produces sixteen-inch stems topped with clusters of fragrant blooms.

RANUNCULUS

Among all the spring bulbs, ranunculuses are the most rewarding for bouquet making. Unlike tulips and narcissus, ranunculuses keep putting forth more and more buds, each plant flowering for several weeks or longer, giving the gardener an ongoing flow of blooms. In bouquets, ranunculuses, whose color range is from purest white to shocking orange and deep rose, with bright yellows, golds, and pastel pinks in between, blend easily with the other flowers and shrubs of spring, or stems can be used on their own.

Although there are about two hundred fifty species of ranunculus, it is the Persian ranunculuses *(Ranunculus asiaticus)* that are grown for cut flowers. In the early part of the twentieth century, breeders developed a strain called Tecolote, which produces large, double, and semidouble camellialike blooms, and whose petals do not scatter in the wind as did those of the older, unimproved strains.

For years, Tecolote ranunculuses have been the standard for cut flowers, with the most exceptional blossoms being produced by bulbs at least five to six inches in circumference, labeled 5/6, and even larger blossoms grown from bulbs of 6/7 and 7-plus sizes.

Ranunculuses can also be grown from seed, but this is not as easy as growing them from bulbs. The seed requires temperatures of 50 to 60 degrees F for fifteen to twenty days in order to germinate, and at least four months and up to six months for blooms to appear, almost twice as long as bulb-grown plants.

The tuberous bulbs have an odd appearance, looking like small shriveled claws. They can be soaked for twenty-four hours before planting to hasten sprouting. In mild winter climates, plant the bulbs from November through February, but in areas with winter freezes, plant them in early spring. They may also be started indoors and later transplanted into the garden.

The planting location should have all-day sun, although some shade may be tolerated. When I have planted them in an area that receives partial shade, the stems have elongated to well over two feet as they reached for the light. The soil should have good drainage, as the bulbs are subject to rot if they are heavy. Ranunculuses will naturalize in areas with mild winter climates, and if that is your desire, plant them six inches apart, allowing them room to spread. If you are treating them as an annual, plant them only two or three inches apart to achieve a massed effect of color. The bulbs should be planted with the claws or fingers pointing downward, and the crown, the flat surface, two inches beneath the soil surface.

Water the bulbs at the time of planting, and then again after the first sprouts appear. Overwatering before a plant's roots have developed may cause the bulb to rot. Water again as needed to keep the ground moist, but not soggy. Winter and spring rains are generally adequate, although as spring fades and with it the rains, the plants will need water to ensure their continued bloom. Few pests attack ranunculuses, except birds.

LONG-LASTING BOUQUETS

For the longest-lasting bouquets in a house, place them away from intense direct sunlight, such as that found in front of a sunny window. Also, keep them at a distance from heat sources, such as wall heaters, overhead heating vents, fireplaces, and stoves, and from cold-air sources, such as air-conditioning vents.

Cut ranunculuses for bouquets when the buds show color and are just about to open. Once cut, the flowers will continue to open and will last for four to five days in water, or five to seven days with floral preservative.

Ranunculuses may be successfully grown in containers, provided they have very good drainage. Avoid overwatering, but the soil should be kept moist from the time the first shoots appear until the bloom period has ended.

There are several strains of ranunculus available in both mixes and single colors.

Tecolote strain (*Ranunculus asiaticus*) mixed has shades of pastels, plus vibrant oranges, yellows, reds, and gold. Mixes in shades are also available, such as red shades, salmon shades, and white shades. Picotee mix, which is all bicolors in all shades, is available as well. The flowers are born on stems from twelve to sixteen inches long.

French Peony (*R. asiaticus*) is similar to the Tecolote strain both in appearance and color, but the stems are somewhat thicker.

Simple Backyard Gardens

A Tulip and Daffodil Garden

In order to have tulips and daffodils for mixed bouquets, it is necessary to plant lots of bulbs that bloom at the same time. Some varieties of both plants bloom early, others midseason, and still others late, so keep this in mind when choosing your bulbs. It is discouraging to plant bulbs while imagining handfuls of orange tulips in bouquets with salmon and white daffodils, only to discover later that the tulip bloom is over before the daffodil begins.

Review the sections in the introduction on planting to prepare the garden ground. For specific information on growing, maintaining, and cutting tulips and daffodils, refer to the "Artful Forms" chapter.

Prepare a garden site of five by nine feet. Using a bulb planter, if desired, plant the daffodil varieties suggested below, keeping the varieties separated. Plant them right next to one another, touching. You will be planting approximately eight or nine bulbs per square foot, closer than recommended by most bulb catalogs because their spacings allow for the bulbs to naturalize and reproduce over time. By planting the bulbs closer together, however, the space is maximized, giving the garden plot a plentiful appearance and allowing you to cut lots of flowers without the plot looking sheared. Follow the daffodil planting with tulips, using the same procedure and spacing.

The bulbs can also be planted in containers in double layers (see page 121).

Water the bulbs well once after planting, and wait for the first green shoots to appear. Then water as needed, although generally winter and spring rains will supply the necessary moisture.

The daffodils and tulips below are all midseason bloomers, but a selection could be made of any number of varieties that bloom at the same time. For successive but fewer blooms per season, select varieties that bloom at different times during the same period.

Plant 48 bulbs of each of the following daffodils:

King Alfred Bright yellow petals with a long trumpet on a sixteen-inch stem.

Professor Einstein White petals with a long, red-orange cup on a fifteen-inch stem.

Easter Bonnet Creamy white with a long, salmon pink cup on a fifteen-inch stem.

Petit Four White petals with a center of ruffled apricot-rose on a sixteen-inch stem.

Mount Hood Pure white petals with a long white trumpet on a sixteen-inch stem.

Plant 25 bulbs of each of the following tulips:

Triumph Orange Cassini Dark red with orange edges on an eighteen-inch stem.

Triumph Apricot Beauty Rich apricot on an eighteen-inch stem.

Triumph Golden Melody Clear, bright yellow on a twenty-two-inch stem.

Triumph Salmon Pearl Rose with a slight apricot edge on a sixteen-inch stem.

Triumph Varinas Dark rose with silvery white edges on a sixteen-inch stem.

A CONTAINER GARDEN

Five containers placed in a sunny location can provide bouquet flowers and garden color from spring through fall. The sweet peas, nasturtiums, and nigellas will be first to bloom, followed by the bachelor's buttons and sunflowers. Vining sweet peas in deepest maroon and vining bright orange and yellow nasturtiums can be left to cascade and trail, or they can be given support to allow them to grow upward. In either case, their growth habit will add interest to the container garden. An airy mass of nigellas fills another container, blue bachelor's buttons and bright yellow sunflowers two more.

Removing spent blossoms and the developing seedpods is especially important in container plantings to keep the plants growing vigorously and blooming over the longest period of time.

Review the sections in In the Garden on planting with special reference to container planting. For specific information on growing, maintaining, and cutting the particular flowers, refer to the chapters that discuss them.

You will need five containers, each eighteen inches across and at least one foot deep, plus enough potting mix to fill them.

SWEET PEA: one packet of **Royal Family Maroon**.

NASTURTIUM: one packet of **Glorious Gleam**.

NIGELLA *(love-in-a-mist):* one packet of blue **Miss Jekyll**.

BACHELOR'S BUTTON: one packet of dwarf **Baby Blue**.

SUNFLOWER: one packet of **Big Smile**.

A High-Summer Garden

A garden that will bloom from midsummer to fall, full of bright colors, is easily grown. These seeds germinate quickly and grow rapidly, and the dahlias send forth shoots from their buried tubers. Plant the garden in rows, placing the tallest plants on the north side of the garden so as not to shade the smaller ones. In this garden, the tallest plants are the sunflowers, followed by cosmos, zinnias, dahlias, and bachelor's buttons.

Review the sections in the introduction on planting to prepare the garden ground. For specific information on growing, maintaining, and cutting the particular flowers, refer to the chapters that discuss them.

Prepare a garden site of about twenty by ten feet, although a smaller plot is possible. Divide it into ten rows, each one foot wide and separated by a one-foot-wide pathway. Sow two rows of sunflowers, two rows of cosmos, two rows of bachelor's buttons, two rows of zinnias, and two rows of dahlias.

The seeds and tubers below are suggestions. Other colorful summertime varieties can be substituted.

SUNFLOWER: one pack of **Autumn Beauty** and **Sunrich Lemon**.

COSMOS: one packet each of mixed **Sensation** and mixed **Seashell**.

BACHELOR'S BUTTONS: one packet each of mixed colors and tall blue.

ZINNIA: one packet each of mixed **Cactus Flowered Bright Jewels** and mixed **California Giants**.

DAHLIA: ten tubers each of a medium-sized cactus-flowered type and a medium-sized decorative type.

RESOURCES

K. Van Bourgondien & Sons
245 Route 109
P.O. Box 1000
Babylon, NY 11702-9004
(800) 552-9996
(516) 669-1228 fax
blooms@dutchbulbs.com
This company is a large supplier of all kinds of bulbs, including bearded irises and perennial plants. Its catalog is illustrated with lush color photography. Free catalog.

McClure & Zimmerman
108 West Winnebago
P.O. Box 368
Friesland, WI 53935
(414) 326-4220
(800) 692-5864 fax
A supplier of bulbs of all kinds, including numerous species tulips

and daffodils, this company prints a catalog beautifully illustrated with botanical drawings. Free catalog.

Swan Island Dahlias
P.O. Box 700
Canby, OR 97013
(503) 266-7711
(503) 266-8768 fax
A large grower of dahlia tubers, Swan Island has an excellent range of classifications and colors. The catalog has beautiful color photography. Catalog costs $3.

Thompson & Morgan
P.O. Box 1308
Jackson, NJ 08527-0308
(908) 363-2225
(908) 363-9356 fax

Although the catalog includes vegetable as well as flower seeds, the flower seeds take up 80 percent of the listings in a publication that generally runs more than 200 pages. Illustrations are full-color photographs. Here one finds seeds for many unusual flowers. Free catalog.

Van Englen Inc.
23 Tulip Drive
Bantam, CT 06750
(860) 567-8734
(860) 567-5323 fax
This supplier has a wide selection of bulbs that are sold only in large minimum lots of 50 or 100. The catalog is illustrated with line drawings. Free catalog.

BIBLIOGRAPHY

Armitage, Allan M. *Specialty Cut Flowers.* Portland, Oregon: Varisty/Timber Press, 1993.

Griffiths, Mark. *Index of Garden Plants: The New Royal Horticultural Society Dictionary of Garden Plants.* London: The Macmillan Press Ltd., 1994.

Hortus Third Dictionary. New York: Macmillan, 1976.

Hunter, Norah T. *The Art of Floral Design.* Albany, New York: Delmar Publications, 1993.

Price, Molly. *The Iris Book.* New York: Dover Publications, 1973.

Spry, Constance. *Simple Flowers.* London: J. M. Dent & Sons, Ltd., 1957.

Sunset Western Garden Book. Menlo Park, California: Sunset Books, 1995.

Index

ACKNOWLEDGMENTS

A special thanks to all the people who helped us create this book:

Thanks to Antonio Huerta Ortega for his help, advice, and concern that he brings to flower growing; to Charlotte Kimball for cuttings, containers, and advice; to Jim Schrupp for reading and rereading the manuscript; to Sharon Silva, the ultimate editor; and to our agent, Susan Lescher, who kept this project moving forward.

Thank you to Kathryn's good friends Amanda Marcus, Stephanie Greenleigh, and Nancy Green for sharing their homes and belongings, and to Jackie Jones for all of her garden support. Thank you to Sonoma Country Pine Antiques' owners Selma and Howard Aslin, and their staff, Britta Borth, Tehra Braren, Patty Ciuca, and JudiAnne Freund for contributing your wonderful antiques and for letting us use your store as a backdrop for photography. Thank you to Carrie Brown and John Werner of Jimtown Store, Healdsburg, California, for allowing us to photograph in the fabulous country setting of your home and store; and to Lynn Scott and Judy Blair of L. Scott and Co., and Suzi Elgin of Kisetsu, both of San Anselmo, California, who lent us unique containers and accessories that helped to make this book special.

Thank you to all who so generously opened their gardens to us: Bonnie Yuill-Thornton of Dragonfly Farms; Tom Ferrell; Frances Andrews and Nigel Walker of Eatwell Farms; Chris and Carmen Rojo of Winters, California; Cynthia Welsh; with a special thanks to Helie Roberston for giving us unlimited access to her enchanting garden.

Thank you to Sarah Zwerling for assisting Ethel with flowers.

Thank you to our Chronicle team for their encouragement and dedication to this project: our editors Leslie Jonath and Bill LeBlond, Pamela Geismar in the art department, and our designer, Gretchen Scoble.

AND SPECIALLY FROM KATHRYN

Thank you to my photo team: Erin Toddhunter, Caroline Kopp, and Kirstie Laird, for their assistance in the studio and on location; and to Teresa Retzlaff, studio manager, who guided me through this project with her garden expertise and her management skills. I could not have completed a year's worth of work without her support.